Soups
& Stews
for Fall and
Winter Days

ALSO FROM BERKSHIRE HOUSE PUBLISHERS

The New Red Lion Inn Cookbook
Suzi Forbes Chase

The Kripalu Cookbook: Gourmet Vegetarian Recipes
Atma Jo Ann Levitt

Apple Orchard Cookbook
Janet Christensen & Betty Bergman Levin

Soups & Stews
for Fall and Winter Days

LIZA FOSBURGH

BERKSHIRE HOUSE PUBLISHERS
Lee, Massachusetts

Library of Congress Cataloging-in-Publication Data

Fosburgh, Liza.
      Soups and stews for fall and winter days / Liza Fosburgh.
            p. cm.
      Includes index.
      ISBN 1-58157-013-9
            1. Soups. 2. Stews. I. Title.

TX757.F67   2000
641.8'13' — dc21

                                                                                  00-030412

ISBN: 1-58157-013-9

Cover design: Jane McWhorter, Blue Sky Productions.
Book design: Liza Fosburgh and Jane McWhorter.

Berkshire House books are available at substantial discounts for bulk
purchases by corporations and other organizations for promotions and
premiums. Special personalized editions can also be produced in large
quantities. For more information, contact:

BERKSHIRE HOUSE PUBLISHERS
480 Pleasant St., Suite 5, Lee, MA 01238
800-321-8526
E-mail: info@berkshirehouse.com
Website: www.berkshirehouse.com

Printed in the United States of America
10 9 8 7 6 5 4 3 2 1

Contents

PART I: MEATS & POULTRY

PART II: BEANS, PEAS, & LENTILS

Cook's Preface

I grew up in a day and age in the deep South when help was fairly commonplace. And in that era, I was fortunate to live in a household where we enjoyed the advantages of this help. However, when I reached adulthood, not only was having help a thing of the past, but I realized there were also certain disadvantages of having grown up with it — one being that I had never even boiled water in the kitchen, let alone cooked a meal. I knew how to stack cream-cheese-and-jelly on soda crackers, and my brother always said I made the best peanut-butter-and-banana sandwiches (which meant I always had to do them), but there it stopped.

My mother was said to be a wonderful cook, but in all truthfulness, I never saw her in the kitchen preparing an entire meal. I remember that she liked to make soups and apple dumplings, and I did see her working on these, with the cook standing off to the side rolling her eyes as she watched the mess grow.

But the soups and dumplings were delicious, and when I reached New York and started working, I decided to learn how to make soup, thinking it sounded the easiest. At least it was something with which I was familiar, and I had always liked it.

My first venture was with cream of mushroom, dictated as I volunteered to contribute that for a joint Thanksgiving meal with friends. I had to buy a cookbook, pot, knife, cutting board, and flour along with the mushrooms and other necessary ingredients (I already had a can opener). It took many hours of preparation, much longer than it should have due to my total lack of experience, but it turned out to be terrific, and it set me off on a pleasure trip into the world of soups.

Over the years, I broadened my cooking repertoire, eventually to extend from appetizers to desserts, but I never stopped making soups. I have gone from standard soups to adventurous soups, from long soups to short-cut soups. We have had meals of soups, first courses of soup, even soups for breakfast, though this was met with so much scepticism I hastily gave it up.

Soups seemed to be particularly fitting to our way of life. For many years now, I have lived in the country, two miles up a dirt road, in an old remodeled farmhouse that is tucked at the base of a mountain. There are big fields that slope away from the sharp mountain grade and that are ideal for sledding. There are old logging trails throughout the surrounding woods that we use for cross-country skiing. There are two big ponds that we clear of snow and use for ice-skating. And always, after any of these activities, a big pot of hot warming soup is welcome.

With fires burning in fireplaces and wood stoves, we sit comfortably around the table with our steaming bowls and don't especially care if the wind begins to howl outside and the sleet starts to strike the windowpanes. We have better things to think about and talk about, especially with pungent aromas rising to nourish and cheer us.

Introduction

The recipes in this book are for the busy do-it-yourself cook/hostess/mother rolled into one who knows ahead of time that at some point on a cold winter's day the kitchen will teem with hungry adults and kids who will be warmed, cheered, and nourished with a hearty hot soup.

With few exceptions, the adults are usually the adventurous ones while the kids are apt to greet every liquidy bowl with a wary eye and suspicious nature that seem to come with birth. It takes too much time to prepare two entirely separate meals for the double-age group, but with a little adjusting and some ambiguous language, you can get away with appealingly satisfactory results for all.

There are a few basic words of advice: Most kids don't like the color green in their cooked food stuffs, especially if it's floating in liquid. I've had my own children eat raw lettuce and celery with abandon, but when it came to a small leaf of kale or spinach in a bowl of soup, their eyes would narrow to slits and their nostrils would curl as they asked "What is that?" while pointing a tiny finger at the steaming culprit. Now they are grown up and have become the adults at table, but there's a new generation coming along with those same eyes and nostrils and stubborn jaws that lock shut no matter how hungry they are. It's a lot easier to make the necessary adjustments ahead of time and be the one to come out on top with everyone eagerly eating and asking for seconds and praising the cook. Bliss.

Serving Tips

Many of these soups, especially those under Meats & Poultry, Beans, Peas, & Lentils, and Seafood, are meals in themselves. They are equally satisfying at lunchtime or dinnertime. To make a fuller meal, serve with hot rolls or biscuits or a loaf of dense crusty grain bread, a light salad, and some cheese and follow with dessert.

Serve these chunky soups in a large soup plate and be generous. If you have a handsome tureen, ladle out the soup at the table. It's an informal way of entertaining and one that all ages like.

With some of the lighter soups, the creamy bisques and purées that are to be served as a first course, try sitting the kids around the kitchen table with a small cup of soup. This has a calming effect that helps maintain a pleasant equilibrium throughout the main meal to follow. Meanwhile, as the little ones are having their soup, attend to the adults. Pass cups of soup right in the living room before dinner, during the tail end of the cocktail hour. This is also an informal way of doing things, but guests seem to like it. The nondrinker or one-cocktail person is especially glad to see real food coming up, and it simplifies serving and clearing the table. As I happen to be the waitress as well as the cook, this takes a big load off my work. However, if you're feeling sprightly, it's certainly nice to have the soup course at the table, served in a pretty soup plate, cream-soup bowl, or bouillon cup.

The number of servings in a recipe depends on how hungry the diners are. Serve in half-cup or whole-cup amounts or save some for seconds. Approximate amounts are listed at the end of the recipes. Remember that rapid boiling without a lid will reduce the amount. Cooks beware!

Meats & Poultry

The onset of winter — those early, crisp days of frost on the window panes and vaporous streams of breath when talking outside — brings out the first awareness that soon the skis and poles will come out of the attic, snowshoes and skates located, and plans will turn to afternoons, weekends, and vacations involving cold outdoor activities. Wood supplies will be checked to make sure there's enough for the season, and chimneys will be cleaned. Mittens, sun goggles, and boots will be reviewed and maybe replaced or put on the Christmas list.

When they were younger, my sons wanted to go to nearby ski centers to meet friends and enjoy the camaraderie and to be part of the festivity of crowds that go with the downhill runs. When they got older, they moved on to cross-country skiing, quietly and softly gliding over old logging roads in the woods, enjoying the stillness, noting animal tracks in the snow, dug-up areas near ferns where wild turkeys scratched for food, ends of branches nibbled by browsing deer. They returned home red-cheeked and bright-eyed — and hungry — ready for the warmth of a fire and a satisfying meal, usually guessing I had a big pot of hot soup on the stove.

If I had ever dared suggest a nice light meal of bouillon and salad, they would have looked at me askance, thinking I had taken leave of my senses. Instead, I, too, thought of "meat-and-potato" pots, hearty fare that goes hand-in-glove with cold outdoors and warm rooms, wood piles and blazing fires, darkening days and long nights. Ah, yes, I, too, thought of the joys of a hearty meaty soup!

Cream Chicken with Avocados

One cooking pot will work for both adults and children. This is a good way to use up some leftover cooked chicken, dark or white.

    2 tablespoons vegetable oil
    2 tablespoons flour
    2 cups chicken stock or canned chicken broth, heated
    1 cup cooked cubed chicken (canned cooked chicken meat can be
        used if you don't have leftovers)
    ¼ teaspoon mace
    ½ cup whole milk
    ½ cup minced or grated carrots
    1 ripe avocado, peeled and thinly sliced for garnish

Heat oil and add flour to make a roux. Gradually add 1 ½ cups of the hot chicken stock, stirring constantly until slightly thickened. Stir in the chicken meat and the mace and simmer gently for a few minutes. Put chicken and stock through blender or food processor to purée. Return to pot and add milk; reheat. In another saucepan, cook the carrots in the remaining ½ cup chicken stock over high heat until barely cooked and still a little crunchy (very few minutes, depending on size of pieces.) Add carrots and stock to chicken mix. Season to taste. Serve hot.

Pass a small plate of avocado slices to the adults for garnish.

Makes about 5 cups.

Excellent with hot buttered biscuits.

Corny Chicken Soup

This is one of those make-ahead soups that can be kept hot for hours on a low burner with a flame protector, without any damage to the quality of the soup. Some kids might have an aversion to lima beans, but they all like corn; if the beans are more or less hidden by the other ingredients, they'll probably be eaten without being noticed.

> 1 small fryer (2 to 2 ½ pounds) or 3 or 4 quartered leg-and-thigh sections
> 6 to 7 cups water
> 1 onion, sliced
> 1 carrot, cut up
> 1 teaspoon each parsley, crumbled bay leaf, and thyme
> few peppercorns
> 2 cups lima beans, fresh or frozen (not dried)
> 2 cups corn, scraped from ears (about 4 ears) or use frozen or canned drained niblets, mashed with a fork
> 4 canned pimientos, finely chopped
> ¼ cup almonds, blanched, peeled, and slivered
> ½ cup shredded coconut, toasted in oven (optional)
> 2 teaspoons Worcestershire sauce

Put chicken pieces and water in a large pot with the onion, carrot, herbs, and peppercorns. Simmer, covered, for about 40 minutes or until chicken is tender. Remove chicken pieces and set aside. Strain liquid through a sieve or colander and reserve the liquid; discard the rest. Skin chicken and remove meat from bones. (Discard skin and bones.) Cut up the meat into small pieces. Return meat and liquid to kettle. Add remaining ingredients. Simmer another 15 to 20 minutes or until beans are soft. Season to taste. Serve hot.

Makes about 12 cups.

Cheesey Chicken

I never knew a youngster to dislike cheese or the flavor of it.

> 1 tablespoon oil, vegetable or olive
> 1 clove garlic, minced
> 1 small onion, minced
> 2 tablespoons minced fresh parsley leaves (dried ones if desperate)
> 4 tablespoons grated Parmesan cheese, preferably fresh
> 1 tablespoon flour
> 3 cups chicken stock or canned chicken broth, heated

In a saucepan, sauté garlic and onion in oil until golden. Add cheese and parsley. Stir in flour and mix well (it will be dense and sticky.) Gradually add hot stock, stirring, and cook until slightly thickened. Season to taste. Serve hot.

To make this a thicker cheese-and-chicken bisque, save out a cup of the chicken stock and purée some cooked chicken meat in it, then add to soup as a final step before seasoning. Yummy, and a big hit with all ages.

Makes about 4 cups.

Clear Duck Soup

Little ones should like the name, and earlier generations with a fond-
ness for old movies might be reminded of that wonderful Marx Broth-
ers gem. This is a clear soup that is ideally used for a first course. The
duck should be used for two meals: the breast meat for an elegant
dinner, and the bones and skin for the soup.

> 1 duckling
> 1 stalk celery, with leaves, cut up
> ½ orange, cut up
> 1 medium onion, sliced
> 6 to 8 cloves
> ¼ teaspoon peppercorns
> 2 teaspoons salt
> 1 teaspoon each parsley, bay leaf, thyme
> water (a quart or more)
> sherry

Split the duckling. Cut out wings and backbone; cut off excess fat. Store
these in the refrigerator until ready to make the soup. Cook the breast
and legs of the duck for dinner, saving the bones and pan drippings for
the soup. To make soup: Combine the uncooked pieces, fat, cooked
bones, and pan drippings in a pot. Add the remainder of the ingredients, using enough water to cover well. Bring to a boil, reduce heat,
cover pot, simmer for 2 to 2 ½ hours. Strain through a fine sieve or
cheesecloth. Cool. Remove all fat from top. Reheat soup, season to
taste, add sherry. Serve hot.

Makes about 5 or so cups.

*If you want to make this a more substantial course, add some hot cooked rice to each soup
cup or bowl. Brown rice would be an excellent choice.*

Green Noodles and Ham

Children who love Dr. Seuss will be more than willing to try this.

    1 ham bone
    3 quarts stock (beef, chicken, or vegetable)
    3 medium onions, quartered
    1 teaspoon peppercorns
    1 teaspoon whole cloves
    1 clove garlic
    2 cups green beans, cut in small pieces (fresh or frozen)
    2 cups green noodles, broken in pieces
    2 cups fresh baby lima beans (or 1 package frozen ones)
    3 stalks celery, chopped
    1 tablespoon Worcestershire sauce
    2 teaspoons prepared horseradish
    ¼ cup sherry

In a large pot, combine first six ingredients. Bring to a boil, reduce heat, cover, simmer for 2 hours. Strain. Dice any pieces of meat left on bone and return to stock. Add remaining ingredients, except sherry. Bring to a boil, reduce heat, and simmer until vegetables and noodles are done, about 15 minutes. Add a little sherry to each bowl for the adults. (If the kids feel cheated, add a little apple juice to their bowls.) Serve hot.

Makes about 18 or 19 cups.

Ham 'n Eggs

Not for breakfast, but a good way to use up some leftover cooked ham. It makes a nice lunch, served with a green salad and Italian bread, and some seedless grapes on the side. (Most children don't like the ones with seeds.)

2 tablespoons oil or butter or margarine
1 green pepper, seeded and finely chopped
2 stalks celery, finely chopped
1 clove garlic, minced
1 cup ground or minced cooked ham
1 tablespoon mustard
2 cups beef stock, heated
2 egg yolks (or use the frozen egg substitute)

In the top of a double boiler, over direct low heat, heat oil (or butter) and sauté the green pepper, celery, and garlic until they are soft. Stir in the ham and mustard. Remove from heat. Beat the egg yolks until frothy. Add a little of the hot stock to them. Add a little more. Then stir the egg mixture into the remainder of the stock, stirring to blend well. Add the stock-egg mix to the ham mix. Place pot over simmering water in bottom of double boiler. Cook, stirring, until slightly thickened. (Be careful not to overcook.) Season to taste. Serve hot.

Makes 4 cups.

Lamb Lovers' Soup

This is a gently flavored, hearty soup, especially good when there's frost on the pumpkin and icicles hanging from the eaves. Use shoulder lamb chops or other cuts with bones and meat. Leftover cooked lamb may be used, but it won't have quite as rich a flavor as starting with raw ingredients. If asked by little ones what is in the soup, it's okay to admit barley.

If you have grown-ups who like lamb kidneys, adapt this recipe to them, substituting kidneys for the chops or leftovers, (taking pains not to mention the word "kidneys" in front of the kids). This is a particularly good and unusual soup, and kidney-lovers will be well rewarded. However, lamb kidneys are hard to find in markets these days. Years ago, they were in any butcher shop; now they're scarce. (Don't use beef kidneys for this; they're too strong.)

> 4 shoulder lamb chops (or 4 lamb kidneys plus about 1 ½ pounds raw lamb bones from butcher) or about 1 ½ cups leftover cooked lamb
> water to cover chops (or bones if using kidneys) or cooked meat, about 3 or 4 cups
> ½ cup pearl barley
> 2 tablespoons vegetable oil
> 1 carrot, diced
> 1 stalk celery, with leaves, diced
> 1 small white turnip, peeled and diced
> 1 onion, chopped
> ½ teaspoon basil
> ¼ teaspoon ground allspice
> parsley for garnish (for adults)

Put the shoulder chops (or bones or cooked meat) in a pot and cover with water. Bring to a boil; stir in the pearl barley. Reduce heat and simmer for 1 ½ hours.

Meanwhile, sauté the vegetables in the oil until they are soft. Remove from heat and set aside. (If using lamb kidneys, skin and remove fatty central part. Cut kidneys into small cubes. Push aside the sautéed vegetables and add kidneys to the pan; cook briefly, stirring, until kidneys are just done — about 5 minutes. Remove pan from heat.

Remove kidneys from pan and set aside.) When barley and chops (or raw bones if used) have finished simmering, remove bones and skim off any fat from liquid. Cut meat off bones and return to liquid. Add vegetables to pot.

(Now is the time to divide the soup if you're using kidneys and you think the kids will reject them. Put half the soup in a separate pot for them. Add the kidneys to the pot for grown-ups. If you have really adventurous youngsters, give them some kidneys, too.) Add basil and allspice. Season to taste. Heat the pot (or two pots) for about 5 minutes. Serve hot, with chopped parsley as a garnish for adults only.

Makes about 5 cups.

Meatball Madness

During college years and after, my sons always came for a long winter
weekend in February, bringing a houseful of friends to skate on the
ponds, go sledding, snowshoe or cross-country ski through the trails we
keep open in the woods. They were always wet, cold, thirsty, and hungry
when they came in at midday and again in the late afternoon. A good
hearty soup hit the spot for the midday break on these weekends.

Now they come with children and bring friends who have children,
and while they might not be quite as hungry and thirsty as they were a
few years ago, they still want the midday soup pot to be bubbling. Little
ones will like this hearty soup, especially once they see the meatballs
swimming in the bowl.

    1 pound ground lean beef
    2 teaspoons salt
    1 teaspoon ground cinnamon
    1 teaspoon sage
    2 tablespoons parsley, minced
    2 tablespoons vegetable oil
    2 tablespoons flour
    l medium onion, chopped
    2 cups chicken stock, heated
    ½ teaspoon thyme
    1 clove garlic, minced and crushed
    1 cup carrots, shredded
    1 quart beef consommé (homemade or use canned consommé)
    4 cups cabbage, finely chopped
    ½ cup dry white wine (beer is an acceptable substitute)
    ½ cup apple juice

Mix the ground beef, salt, cinnamon, sage, and parsley. Shape it into
tiny meatballs, about as big as a large marble, and sauté them in oil in a
deep pot. When meatballs are done, remove them and set aside. In the
drippings in the pot, sauté the onion over low heat until golden.
Sprinkle on the flour and mix well. Stir in the hot chicken stock, stirring, and cook gently until it slightly thickens. Add the thyme, garlic,
carrots, and consommé. Scrape up any bits sticking at the bottom of
the pot and stir well. Simmer until carrots are just tender, about 10

minutes. Add the cabbage and cook another 5 minutes or until cabbage is tender but still a little crispy. Return meatballs to pot and mix well.

Take out half the soup and put into another pot for the kids. Add the white wine to the pot for adults and the apple juice to the pot for kids. Season both to taste. Serve hot.

Makes 3-plus quarts.

The addition of a cup of diced potatoes, at same time as the carrots, makes this soup even heartier.

Mulligatawny

Children like the name; everyone likes the soup.

    4 tablespoons oil, vegetable or olive

    2 onions, chopped

    2 carrots, thinly sliced

    1 apple, peeled, cored, and chopped

    2 stalks celery, chopped

    ¼ pound mushrooms, chopped

    2 tablespoons fresh parsley, minced

    2 tablespoons flour

    ½ teaspoon thyme

    1 bay leaf, crushed

    1 ½ quarts chicken stock, heated (lamb stock may be substituted)

    ½ cup whole milk

    1 cup cooked chicken meat, diced (or lamb)

    1 ½ teaspoons curry powder

    hot cooked rice

Heat oil and sauté vegetables over low heat until soft. Stir in flour, thyme, and bay leaf. Gradually add the hot stock, stirring until slightly thickened. Cover and simmer 15 minutes.

    Purée in blender or food processor. Divide into two pots, one for adults and one for kids. Add ¼ cup milk to each pot; add ½ cup chicken (or lamb) to each pot. From pot for adults, lift out a little soup and stir in the curry powder, mixing until smooth. Return to pot. Heat both pots and serve soup over rice.

Makes 9 or so cups.

If your little ones like the curry flavor, keep everything in one pot and double amount of curry powder, to 1 tablespoon.

Noodle Slurp

Not the most appetizing name, but it certainly describes it. I prefer the very thin noodles for this, but certainly the broader ones can be used. Good crusty French bread or hard rolls make wonderful "pushers."

> 2 tablespoons oil, olive or vegetable
> 1 onion, chopped
> 1 sweet green pepper, seeded and chopped
> ¼ pound mushrooms, chopped
> 2 or 3 large ripe tomatoes, peeled and chopped
>   (or use canned ones)
> ½ cup cooked corn, scraped from cob
>   (or use cream-style canned corn)
> ¼ cup ripe black olives, pitted and minced
> 1 quart chicken stock
> ½ cup cooked cubed chicken meat (or use canned boned chicken)
> 1 box thin angel noodles

Sauté onion, pepper, and mushrooms in oil until soft. Add remaining ingredients, except noodles. Bring to simmering and cook gently for 30 minutes. Meanwhile, in a separate pot, cook the noodles according to package directions. Drain. Add to soup. Season to taste. Serve hot.

Makes 6 or 7 cups.

A Pot of Pepperoni

Terrific . . . and a hit with hungry big or little diners.

>   1 clove garlic, minced and crushed
>   1 tablespoon oil, olive or vegetable
>   ½ cup onion, chopped
>   ⅓ cup chopped pepperoni
>   1 1-pound 12-ounce can crushed tomatoes
>   3 cups chicken stock
>   ½ teaspoon basil
>   ½ teaspoon oregano
>   1 teaspoon parsley, minced
>   ¼ teaspoon red-pepper flakes
>   1 1-pound can garbanza beans, rinsed and drained
>   ½ 10-ounce package frozen kale
>   or collard greens, thawed and drained
>   hot cooked rice

In a large kettle, sauté garlic and onion in oil until soft and golden. Add pepperoni, tomatoes, stock, herbs, and red-pepper flakes. Bring to a boil, reduce heat, and simmer for 15 minutes. Add garbanza beans and simmer all together for about 10 minutes. Divide soup into two pots. Add the kale or collard greens to the pot for adults; cook for 10 or 15 minutes or until greens are tender. Serve hot over some hot cooked rice in bottom of each soup bowl.

Makes 10 to 12 cups.

Red Cabbage Patch Soup

Cabbage is a mystery vegetable with children. Some like it; some don't. When they were younger, one of my sons claimed it be to his favorite vegetable; the other one ate it under protest. Red cabbage might be more appealing than green to the young, especially if it is cooked with a rich and pungent stock. It certainly is worth a try, and the chances are that the kids will like it. A dark, dense grainy bread goes very well with this.

> 2 tablespoons vegetable oil
> 2 onions, chopped
> 1 clove garlic, minced
> 1 pound lean beef, cubed
> 2 tablespoons flour
> 2 cups beef stock, heated
> 2 cups finely shredded red cabbage
> 1 tablespoon sugar
> 1 teaspoon vinegar
> 1 cup beer
> 1 cup ginger ale
> ½ teaspoon thyme
> ½ teaspoon crumbled bay leaf

Heat oil in a large kettle. Add and brown the onions, garlic, and beef. Sprinkle on the flour; mix well. Gradually add the hot beef stock, stirring, and cook until slightly thickened. Stir in the sugar and vinegar. Lift out half and put into a separate pot for the kids.

Into the original cooking kettle, now the one for adults, add the beer, ¼ teaspoon thyme, and ¼ teaspoon bay leaf. Into the second pot for kids, add the ginger ale, remaining thyme and bay leaf. Bring both pots to a boil, reduce heat, cover, and simmer for 1 hour or more, until beef is tender and flavors blended. Season to taste. Serve hot.

Makes about 9 cups.

Southern Vegetable

This is really an old-fashioned Southern okra soup, given to me by the late Savannah-born Claudia McAlpin Whitney. It was a house specialty of hers and everyone loved it. However, when feeding kids, it's best to call it a Southern vegetable soup and avoid any unpleasant conversation about the merits of okra.

>   2 ½ pounds beef brisket (not too fat), cut in small pieces
>   1 quart vegetable stock (or chicken stock or canned chicken broth may be used)
>   2 cups peeled and chopped tomatoes (or use canned Italian plum tomatoes, drained)
>   1 green pepper, seeded and chopped
>   4 cups young fresh okra, stem end removed and okra cut in small pieces (very small, if dealing with fussy kids)
>   1 cup fresh corn (or use frozen corn, thawed and drained)
>   1 cup fresh or frozen lima beans
>   hot cooked rice

Combine beef, stock, tomatoes, green pepper, and okra. Slowly bring to a boil, reduce heat, cover, and simmer about 2 hours. Add corn and lima beans. Cook another 30 minutes or more. Season to taste. Serve hot over rice. Scrumptious.

Makes 3 to 4 quarts.

Beans, Peas, & Lentils

Beans are protein-rich and good alternatives to meaty dishes. Delicious, too. This is especially true after the holidays, when turkey seems to be a month-long staple between Thanksgiving and Christmas and when every party buffet table features baked ham. A switch to beans is a welcome change.

When I was a child in the South, baked beans were very popular — and almost ubiquitous at picnics, barbecue get-togethers, and church socials. This was true in other parts of the country, too. In many places, baked beans still are very popular (and still good), but they now have a lot of company with other bean dishes.

When my sons were young, they early on liked exotic bean dishes such as a Spanish favala and French cassoulet, great concoctions calling for varieties of the white-bean family. Black-eyes peas next were accepted in wonderful Southern dishes. Then came red beans. Lastly came black beans, but they did come. By the time they finished college and were on their own, learning to cook and to entertain on a budget, they became experimental with many beans and other legumes. We even grew soy beans in the vegetable garden one summer — delicious when picked young, but difficult to shell and not tried the second year.

The following recipes are long-standing favorites in my family, and we now want to share them with all ages.

Black and Spicy Bean

The dark color should not bother kids— after all, they're accustomed to chocolate pudding. But it will certainly be best to leave the hot spices in the pot for adults only.

> 1 cup dried black bans, soaked according to package directions
> 1 quart water
> ham bone or lamb bone, if available (if not, cut up 2 or 3 slices of bacon into the water pot)
> 1 stalk celery, chopped
> 1 carrot, chopped
> ½ onion, chopped
> 1 teaspoon lemon juice
> 1 bay leaf
> ½ teaspoon dry mustard
> 1 teaspoon Worcestershire sauce
> ½ teaspoon chili powder, plus a pinch
> ¼ teaspoon hot red-pepper sauce
> thin slices of lemon for garnish

Drain soaked beans and add to water in a large pot with the bone (or bacon), celery, carrot, onion, lemon juice, bay leaf, dry mustard, and Worcestershire sauce. Cover tightly. Bring to simmer and cook slowly over low heat for 3 hours or more, until beans are very soft. (If too much liquid should be absorbed, add a little more water. This will depend on heaviness of pot, tightness of lid, and amount of cooking heat.) Remove bone; skim off any fat from top. Put all through blender or food processor to purée. Divide into two pots, one for adults and one for kids. To soup for the former, add ½ teaspoon chili powder and the ¼ teaspoon hot pepper sauce. To soup for little ones, add a small pinch of chili powder, maybe an ⅛ teaspoon. Bring back to simmer and cook, both pots, for about 10 minutes. Season to taste with salt if needed. Serve hot, with thin slices of lemon for adults.

Makes 5 to 6 cups.

Black-eyed Pea Soup

In the deep South, this soup is called "Hog Jowl and Pea Soup," and it is traditional to eat it on New Year's Day. It is said to bring good luck for the rest of the year. I'm not sure where this custom started, (though I believe it is French in origin, brought to this country by the French Huguenots), but I do know that I am not about to taunt fate and ignore it.

Originally, the jaw bone of a hog was used, but now any old ham bone is acceptable. The dish can be in the thick form of a vegetable potpourri or it can be a soup. In my family, it was always in the soup form. A pot of hog-jowl-and-pea soup was kept on the back of the stove all day, ready to be eaten by visitors who dropped in to exchange New Year's Day greetings — a very nice custom that has unfortunately seen better days.

When my Northern-raised children were little, they had to be coaxed to eat it. Now that they are grown up, they even call on New Year's Eve and ask to be reminded how to make it.

My recipe is very simple, and it is always liked, even by fussy little ones.

    1 pound dried black-eyed peas
    water for soaking peas
    ham stock (ham leg bone or ham knuckle covered with a quart or
        more of water and simmered for an hour or more)
    1 carrot, diced
    2 stalks celery, with leaves, chopped fine
    1 medium onion, chopped

Wash and soak peas according to package directions. When ready to drain, add to ham stock, which you have already made. Add vegetables. Bring to a boil; reduce heat; cover; simmer for about 1 hour or a little more. Add more water if necessary. Test the peas every now and again and remove from heat as soon as they are tender. Be sure not to over-cook — mushy beans are not desirable. Serve hot.

Makes about 8 cups.

A loaf of crusty French or Italian bread is wonderful with this; use it to soak up the juice in the bottom of the soup bowl. Walter Rowland, of Wilmington, always adds a little red hot pepper to his soup. A small bottle of hot-pepper sauce on the table is a nice taste addition to this, for adults only.

Black Eyes and Rice

This is not the lucky soup to be eaten on New Year's Day, but it is another good one made with black-eyed peas and, like plain Black-eyed Pea Soup, can be made for all ages in one cooking pot. It's delicious and hearty for a blustery winter day, lunch or supper.

> 1 1-pound package black-eyed peas
> water for peas
> ¼ pound lean salt pork, cut in small cubes
> 1 tablespoon vegetable oil
> 2 onions, chopped
> 2 quarts beef stock
> 4 or 5 ripe tomatoes, peeled and chopped (or use 1 large 1-pound 12-ounce can of tomatoes, chopped)
> 1 teaspoon oregano
> 1 cup raw white rice

Soak peas in water according to package directions. Drain. Sauté the salt pork in the oil in a heavy pot over very low heat until it is just golden. Add the onions to the kettle and cook until soft. Add the drained beans, beef stock, tomatoes, and oregano. Simmer, covered, for 1 hour. Stir in the rice and simmer for another 25 minutes or until rice is done. Serve hot.

Makes a lot, probably 3 quarts.

Cowboy Bean Soup

This soup has the flavors of the old Southwest and could have been made right at the chuck wagon for those hungry cowboys taking a break from a day on the range. It will go down just as easily for your hungry players in from the cold.

3 tablespoons vegetable oil
2 onions, chopped
3 stalks celery, chopped
½ pound ground beef
1 clove garlic, minced
1 cup canned drained whole-kernel corn
1 large can (1 pound 12 ounces) peeled tomatoes, chopped
1 ½ quarts beef stock (homemade or canned)
2 1-pound cans kidney beans
2 teaspoons chili powder
2 teaspoons ground cumin
1 teaspoon dill seed
1 teaspoon crushed red pepper
½ cup beer
½ cup apple juice

Heat oil in large heavy pot and sauté onions, celery, beef, and garlic. When beef is lightly browned and vegetables soft, add corn, tomatoes, beef stock, beans, chili powder, cumin, and dill seed. Mix well, cover pot, and simmer over low heat for 45 minutes to 1 hour.

Divide soup into two pots. In pot for adults, add red pepper and beer; in pot for kids, add apple juice. Simmer for another 10 minutes. Serve hot.

Makes enough for a crowd, about 4-plus quarts.

Great with cornbread.

Creamy Split Pea

This is really Mongol Soup, but that sounds too strange for little ones.

½ of a 1 pound box of split peas
1 quart water
ham bone or a chunk of salt pork
4 ripe tomatoes, peeled and chopped (or use canned ones)
1 onion, chopped
1 stalk celery with leaves, chopped
1 carrot, scraped and diced
1 clove garlic, minced and crushed (with garlic press or back
    of a spoon)
1 bay leaf, crumbled
½ teaspoon sugar
pinch each of ground cloves and cayenne (maybe ⅛ teaspoon)
1 tablespoon flour
½ cup milk

Wash and drain split peas. Combine with water, ham bone or salt pork, tomatoes, onion, celery, carrot, garlic, bay leaf, sugar, cloves, and cayenne. Bring to a boil; reduce heat; cover and simmer for 1 ½ to 2 hours. Remove bone or salt pork; skim off any fat. Blend together flour, milk, and a little of the hot soup until creamy. Add this to the soup pot and stir well.

Return to simmering and cook another 10 to 15 minutes, stirring occasionally. Put all through blender or food processor. Reheat and serve hot.

Makes about 8 cups.

Kids might like to crumble up some saltine crackers on this.

Curried Split Pea

This mild curry-flavored pea soup is very different from regular split pea. There's not so much spice that the children will object. Pass additional curry powder to big people for a stronger flavor.

    3 tablespoons vegetable or olive oil
    2 medium onions, chopped
    1 clove garlic, minced and crushed
    1 1-pound package dried split peas, washed and drained
    2 ½ quarts water
    1 small 6-ounce can tomato paste
    2 tablespoons mustard seed
    2 teaspoons curry powder
    ½ cup applesauce

In a large pot, sauté onions and garlic in oil until golden. Add remaining ingredients, bring to a boil, reduce heat, cover, and simmer for an hour or more, until peas are quite soft and mushy. Season to taste. Serve hot.

Makes almost 4 quarts.

This is good over hot cooked rice for a bigger meal.

Lentil

One of the old standbys, but it can't be beat as a standing favorite for lunch or supper. I use either a ham bone or a lamb bone, whichever I have in the freezer.

1 1-pound package dried lentils, washed and drained
1 clove garlic, minced
1 onion, chopped
2 carrots, diced
1 small zucchini, diced (optional, but it adds a lot)
1 small can tomato paste
ham or lamb bone
2 quarts water

Combine everything in a deep kettle, bring to simmering, cover, and simmer for 2 to 2 ½ hours. Remove bone and cut off any meat and add to kettle. Season to taste. Serve hot.

Makes about 3 quarts.

Beans and Sausage

This is very hearty and filling, ideally suited for a warm meal in a toasty house after cross-country skiing or vigorous sledding. Serve it with some good dense black bread or grainy bread. All ages.

> 2 1-pound cans of cannellini (white kidney) beans, drained (or use 2 cups dried marrow beans or Great Northern beans, soaked according to package directions and drained)
> 1 pound ground sweet sausage meat
> 2 onions, chopped
> 1 clove garlic, minced
> ½ sweet green pepper, seeded and chopped
> 1 bay leaf, crumbled
> 1 teaspoon dried red-pepper flakes
> 2 quarts beef stock
> 4 ripe tomatoes, peeled and chopped (or canned ones)

In a large heavy pot, brown sausage until it is crumbly. Lift out and set aside. In 2 tablespoons of the drippings in the pot (discard remainder), sauté onions, pepper, and garlic until soft. Return sausage to pot. Add beans and remaining ingredients. Bring to a boil, reduce heat, cover, and simmer for 45 minutes or so (or longer if using dried beans). Skim off any fat. Season to taste. Serve hot.

Makes about 4 quarts.

Easy Minestrone

Easy and good to the last drop. It will be a hit with everyone.

   2 quarts water
   2 teaspoons salt
   1 cup cabbage, chopped
   1 cup green beans, fresh or frozen, cut up
   2 carrots, peeled and sliced thin
   1 large potato, peeled and cubed
   2 turnips, peeled and cubed
   2 slices bacon, cut in small pieces
   1 onion, chopped
   1 stalk celery, chopped, with leaves
   ¼ cup fresh parsley, chopped
   1 clove garlic, minced
   1 cup elbow macaroni
   1 1-pound can Great Northern beans, drained
   1 1-pound can chopped tomatoes
   grated Parmesan cheese, fresh or dried

Into a large heavy pot, put the water, salt, cabbage, green beans, carrots, potato, and turnips. Bring to a boil, reduce heat to simmering, cover and cook for an hour or so. Meanwhile, in a heavy skillet, cook bacon, onion, celery, parsley, and garlic over medium heat, stirring, until vegetables are slightly browned and soft. Add this to the big pot simmering with the vegetables and continue cooking, covered. At the end of the hour (or more), add the macaroni, canned beans, and tomatoes and simmer another 15 minutes or more until macaroni is cooked. Remember that simmering at low heat, covered, gives the individual flavors time to blend and meld into a wonderful whole. Pass the Parmesan cheese as a garnish.

Makes a lot, almost 5 quarts.

Here's a hint if you think you'll be short on chopping time: use a large package of raw cole-slaw vegetables in place of the cabbage and carrots and get the rest of the vegetables in the frozen department of the market.

Southwest Lentil

A delicious variation on the old standby.

 1 cup lentils, rinsed and drained
 6 cups water
 ham bone or lamb bone
 1 green pepper, seeded and diced
 1 onion, chopped
 1 cup fresh or frozen green beans, cut in small pieces
 2 cups canned drained whole-kernel corn
 2 canned pimientos, chopped
 ½ teaspoon chili powder
 ¼ teaspoon cayenne pepper

Combine lentils, water, and bone in a large heavy pot. Bring to a boil, reduce heat, cover, and simmer for 45 minutes. Remove bone and skim off any fat. Add green pepper, onion, green beans, corn, and pimientos. Bring to simmering and cook gently, covered, for another 30 minutes. (If too thick, add a little canned beef bouillon or water and bouillon cube.) Ladle out half into another pot. To pot for adults, add chili powder and cayenne. Serve hot.

Makes 10 to 12 cups.

Split Pea

As in Creamy Split Pea Soup, a ham bone is preferable, but lamb or beef bones are acceptable substitutes in making this soup. Lacking any of these, get a chunk of lean salt pork. If you're a vegetarian, use vegetable stock instead of meat bones and water.

This is quite similar to Creamy Split Pea, but different enough to be included as a separate recipe.

    1 1-pound package dried split peas
    2 ½ quarts boiling water
    ham bone or a chunk of salt pork
    2 onions, chopped
    2 stalks celery, with leaves, chopped
    2 carrots, chopped
    1 clove garlic, minced and crushed
    1 teaspoon marjoram
    1 teaspoon honey
    ¼ teaspoon nutmeg
    dash of cayenne
    1 cup milk
    2 tablespoons flour
    toasted rye-bread croutons for garnish (mainly for adults)

Wash and drain peas. Combine in a large pot with remaining ingredients, except milk, flour, and croutons. Bring to a boil, reduce heat, cover, and simmer for 2 to 2 ½ hours. Remove bone or pork chunk; skim off any fat. In a small bowl, gradually blend the milk with the flour. Add some of the hot soup to this and blend well. Then stir the milk mix into the soup pot and stir well, making sure it blends in. Heat just to simmering and simmer gently for 10 to 15 minutes, stirring several times. Season to taste. Serve hot, with toasted rye croutons.

Makes about 4 quarts.

If you have any leftover soup, you might like to try one of the following quick combinations.

Combine equal amounts of split-pea soup and: chicken or beef broth for a thinner soup; apple juice especially for kids; milk, and consommé; milk, and canned crushed tomatoes; milk with a generous dollop of yogurt

White Bean Soup

White-bean soups are among my family's favorites. Mine, too. There's so much versatility. Once you get the hang of making bean soups, be adventurous and experiment with new ingredients — herbs, vegetables, spices.

    1 onion, finely chopped
    1 stalk celery, with leaves, finely chopped
    2 ripe tomatoes, peeled and cubed (or use canned ones)
    1 tablespoon tomato purée
    1 tablespoon brown sugar
    1 teaspoon dry mustard
    1 teaspoon chili powder
    1 quart water
    1 1-pound can white beans (pea, Great Northern, or chick pea)
    ¼ cup sherry
    ¼ cup apple juice or white grape juice
    fresh cilantro or parsley for garnish (grown-ups only)

In a large heavy pot, combine onion, celery, tomatoes, tomato purée, brown sugar, dry mustard, chili powder, and water. Bring to a boil, reduce heat, cover tightly, and simmer for 45 minutes to an hour to get a good flavorful base. Drain the canned beans and add to soup pot. Simmer another 15 to 20 minutes. Divide soup into two pots. Add sherry to pot for adults; add juice to pot for kids. Garnish with parsley or cilantro for adults. Serve hot.

Makes about 8 cups.

Buttered hot yeast rolls are wonderful with this.

White Beans and Lamb

A good basic bean-and-meat soup, this protein-laden concoction is a wonderful substitute for a meat and vegetable meal — even dinner with family or guests. Served with cornbread, a green salad, and dessert, it's a real meal.

 1 1-pound box Great Northern beans
 water
 2 tablespoons butter or margarine
 1 pound stewing lamb, that has been trimmed of fat and cut
    into cubes (if stewing lamb is not available, use the meat
    from shoulder chops)
 2 small onions, chopped
 lamb bones, weighing about 1 to 1 ½ pounds,
    (cracked, if possible*)
 2 ½ quarts water
 1 carrot, finely diced
 1 tablespoon salt
 a small bouquet garni (about a tablespoon of parsley, bay leaf,
    rosemary, and thyme, all tied in a cloth bag)

Soak beans in water as directed on package. Drain. To make the soup: In a large kettle, melt the butter and brown the lamb meat and the onions. Add the drained beans, bones, 2 ½ quarts water, carrot, salt, and herbs. Bring to a boil, reduce heat, and simmer for about 2 ½ hours or until beans are soft. Remove bones and bouquet garni bag. Season to taste. Serve hot.

Makes a lot, 4 quarts or more.

Note: If you don't mind the herbs floating around in the soup, add a scant ½ teaspoon of each herb instead of bouquet garni in a bag.

*Ask the butcher to crack the bones for you. Though this is not essential in making the soup, the marrow in the bones will provide additional flavor if they are cracked.

Seafood

For the true fisherman, there is no season on thinking of fish — it's a year-round process. But winter is the ideal time to check on fishing gear.

My number-two son began tying wet and dry flies (for trout and other freshwater species) when he was eight years old. By the time he was twelve, he picked up a bit of pocket change selling his handmade flies. One summer when we went to Alaska to fish the waters of the Kenai Peninsula, bringing the boys' best friend, who was like a member of the family, these fly-tying skills proved invaluable and necessary as the many flies we had taken with us were lost to the large salmon slamming onto them and then running away at break-neck speed in the rushing river. Every night, more flies were tied, and the three boys did manage to outwit and out-maneuver many a tasty fish.

After that, number-one son started tying flies — and they both still do, lo, these many years later. The skill and grace in casting a delicate fly far out into the water is always a thing of beauty to see and a skill to appreciate. I sit quietly in a rowboat or on a riverbank and watch and marvel at this graceful wonder of placing a tiny fly exactly where the fish will bite. Most of the time, they release their catches, but occasion-ally we get to eat a nice plump trout. It's always a special treat.

I would never use one of these fish in a soup dish, no matter the season — a sacrilege. But I do like to eat fish soups, so off to the market I go. They are especially good in winter, when catching them in the wild is but a dream.

Easy Bouillabaisse

This is really a Mediterranean fisherman's stew, rather than a traditional soup. Bouillabaisse ingredients may be varied as desired, preferably using both the traditional fish and shellfish, along with tomatoes and onions. However, I say anything goes within reason. Use this recipe as a guide and let your imagination select what's available in your market. Do not worry if purists, who insist on fish and shellfish, look down their noses at your imaginative pot. Once they taste your concoction, they'll smile.

 4 large Spanish onions, sliced
 2 potatoes, peeled and sliced
 3 or 4 ripe tomatoes, peeled and chopped, (or used canned ones)
 2 leeks, chopped
 1 carrot, diced
 1 clove garlic, minced
 2 tablespoons parsley, chopped
 1 teaspoon bay leaf, crumbled into tiny pieces
 ½ teaspoon rosemary
 ½ teaspoon thyme
 1 teaspoon salt
 ½ teaspoon fennel seed
 ½ small (6 ounce) can tomato paste
 ½ cup oil, olive or vegetable
 1 tablespoon lemon juice
 2 cups water
 2 or more pounds boned fish (cod, halibut, mackerel, perch, red snapper, sea bass, flounder, etc. Use a combination of varieties), cut into chunks
 2 small lobsters in shell, or 3 or 4 frozen lobster tails, thawed (or use 1 pound shrimp if lobsters are not available) or use some of the imitation lobster meat found in fish markets
 additional handful of scallops is optional and very rich

In a large heavy pot, combine vegetables and herbs. Mix tomato paste, oil, water, and lemon juice in a separate bowl or large measuring cup and then add to the vegetables. (Easier than trying to blend in paste and oil in same pot with vegetables.) Cover tightly and simmer over very low heat for about 30 minutes or until vegetables are tender. The vegetables will produce juice. (If more water is needed, add a little at a time, but don't get it too watery.)

When vegetables are done, add the fish, lobster, and other seafood you have, placing them right on top of the vegetables. Return pot to simmer. Cover tightly and steam the fish and shellfish, for about 15 to 20 minutes or until lobster has turned red. (If scallops are also used, add them a little later than the fish and lobster.) Remove lobsters and cut them into pieces. Some cooks remove the fish chunks also, but I prefer to leave these in with the vegetables. (Remove shrimp if used). Put shell pieces (lobster or shrimp) on a separate plate.

Serve the soup hot, with the shellfish on the side, letting diners cope with their own shells. This is especially useful if little ones have an aversion to eating things in shells.

Makes a generous 4 quarts.

A thick slice of hot French bread is the best thing to serve with this, for pushing and for sopping up the tasty juice.

Chunky Fish Chowder

Easy—and one cooking pot for all ages. Double recipe for more; halve for less. Nice creamy-white color.

 1 pound fillet of haddock or other sea fish (preferably white)
 1 cup water
 2 cups peeled and cubed potatoes
 1 strip bacon
 1 small onion, chopped
 1 small clove garlic, minced
 1 cup whole milk
 1 cup plain yogurt

In a 2-quart saucepan (or larger), poach fish fillet in the cup of water until it flakes easily, about 4 to 5 minutes. Remove fish, save liquid. Discard skin and any bones from fillet. Flake flesh into small chunks and set aside.

In the fish cooking liquid, simmer potatoes over low heat until tender. Remove from heat and add flaked fish chunks to this saucepan. Set aside. In separate skillet, cook bacon until crisp; remove, crumble and add to potatoes and fish. In bacon drippings, sauté garlic and onion until golden. Add all this to potatoes-and-fish saucepan. Add milk and yogurt; mix well. (Season to taste with salt and pepper as desired.) Reheat almost to simmering (do not let boil). Serve hot.

Makes 8 to 10 cups.

Gumbo of the South

Kids should take to the name, but to be on the safe side, have two pots available. This is based on a traditional Southern soup from the coastal regions of Georgia and South Carolina.

> ¼ pound lean sweet sausage
> 1 to 3 tablespoons vegetable oil
> 1 cup diced ham
> 1 medium onion, chopped
> 1 large green pepper, seeded and chopped
> 1 cup parsley, minced
> 1 stalk celery, with leaves, chopped
> 1 bay leaf, crumbled
> 1 clove garlic, minced
> 1 quart water
> 1 teaspoon salt
> 1 pound shrimp, fresh or frozen
> 1 pint oysters, fresh (shucked and in pint containers in store)
> 2 small cans tomato paste
> 2 tablespoons flour
> 1 pound fresh okra, cut up (or use frozen)
> 2 tablespoons gumbo filé (available in specialty food sections of supermarkets) or use Old Bay Seasoning
> cooked rice

Brown and crumble sausage in a deep heavy pot. Remove and add enough oil to sausage drippings to make 3 tablespoons. Sauté ham until nicely browned; remove from pot and set aside with sausage. To pot with oil, add onion, green pepper, parsley, celery, bay leaf, and garlic. Sauté over low heat until golden. Remove pot from heat and set aside. Bring water to a boil in a separate pot. Add salt. Add shrimp and boil for a few minutes, maybe 5, until shrimp turn pink. Lift out shrimp, set aside; then add oysters to boiling water. Cook oysters, also briefly, until edges begin to curl. Lift out and set aside.

Add the seafood liquid to the big pot with the sautéed vegetables. Add the tomato paste and stir well. Simmer, covered, over low heat for 45 minutes to an hour, to get a rich flavor. Meanwhile, peel and devein shrimp. After vegetables have simmered, gradually mix some of the hot vegetable liquid with the flour in a separate small bowl to make a smooth thin runny paste. Add this to the vegetable pot and mix well. Add chopped okra and gumbo filé (or Old Bay Seasoning). Add ham.

Now is when you have to make a judgment call about your kids and seafood. If in doubt, put the soup into two pots and add the shrimp and oysters to pot for adults only. Serve hot, with some hot cooked rice in bottom of each soup bowl.

Makes about 4 quarts.

Mediterranean Fish Stew

Another fish stew, this one with its origins nearer Spain and Portugal. As with Bouillabaisse, the cook can leave her special mark on this by using her imagination. The following is a good guide. (I've added summer squashes — yellow crooknecks and zucchini — with great success.)

2 pounds fish fillets, boned and cubed, (fresh or frozen)
2 large sweet onions, quartered and sliced or coarsely chopped
2 large potatoes, peeled and coarsely chopped
1 teaspoon salt
1 tablespoon vegetable or olive oil
1 bay leaf, crumbled
tomato juice to cover

In a deep heavy pot with a lid, combine the fish, potatoes, and onions. Sprinkle on the salt, olive oil, and bay leaf. Pour over this enough tomato juice to completely cover the ingredients. (This will depend on the size of the pot.) Cover tightly and simmer gently for about 45 minutes. Season to taste. Serve hot. (If too thick, add more tomato juice.)

All ages will readily eat it. Great with Italian bread for sopping up the last of the juice.

Makes about 8 cups.

Old-fashioned Oyster Stew

When I was a child in the South, there would be great excitement the day the oysters arrived. These were packed in ice in a large wooden barrel (the kind that are now cut in half and used as planters). I never knew where they came from, but remember well the festive air that came with them. I usually hung back at the edges, raw oysters being a bit too adventurous for me, staring in wonder at my father who would place a straight chair next to the barrel in the backyard and begin to shuck and eat. He was usually a man of temperate emotions, but the day the oysters came he would be as excited as the rest of us were on Christmas.

I did like oyster stew though, and some of the oysters were always saved for that. As I was a rather fussy eater and thought this was good, the chances are that your small ones will like it too. Worth a try.

    4 tablespoons butter or margarine
    2 pints oysters with liquid (shucked and in pints in stores)
    1 tablespoon Worcestershire sauce
    1 teaspoon salt
    ¼ teaspoon white pepper (or small pinch of cayenne)
    2 cups whole milk
    2 cups light cream or more whole milk
    toasted oyster crackers

Heat butter in top of double boiler over direct low heat. Add oysters, Worcestershire sauce, salt, and pepper. Cook over very low heat, occasionally stirring, until oyster edges just begin to curl, about 3 to 5 minutes Put pot over boiling water in bottom of double boiler. Add the milk and cream. Heat thoroughly, until the oysters are plump and the edges fully curled. Do not overcook — oysters will get tough. Season to taste. Children will surely like the milky-creamy flavor of the stew; if in doubt about the actual oysters, simply lift them out with a slotted spoon and add to the bowls for the adults. Serve hot with toasted oyster crackers. Little ones love these.

Makes about 8 cups.

Oyster Gumbo

Different from the traditional Southern Gumbo, with a rich piquant flavor.

Serve alone or over hot cooked rice. The question of kids and oysters is again present. You may need two pots.

2 onions, chopped

½ lemon, seeded and minced (peel and all)

2 tablespoons vegetable oil

½ pound mushrooms, thinly sliced

2 cups green beans, cut up (or use frozen, cut up)

1 cup green peas, fresh or frozen

4 or 5 large ripe tomatoes, peeled and chopped (or use canned)

2 tablespoons flour

3 cups chicken stock, heated

1 teaspoon mace

2 teaspoons paprika

1 teaspoon ground cumin seed

1 ½ to 2 pints oysters, (shucked, with liquid, in stores)

In a large heavy pot, sauté onions and lemon in oil until soft and slightly browned. Add mushrooms and sauté 2 to 3 minutes. Add beans, peas, and tomatoes and mix well. Sprinkle on flour and blend in. Gradually add the hot stock, stirring, and cook until slightly thickened. Add spices. Now is the time to use two pots if you think the kids won't like oysters. For them, simply serve hot. For adults, bring soup just to boiling and stir in oysters. Simmer until oyster edges begin to curl, about 3 to 5 minutes. Season to taste. Serve hot.

Makes 3-plus quarts.

Red Clam Chowder

New England clam chowder is still a great soup, but it's best made with lots of butter and cream. As an occasional treat, look up a recipe and make some. For more ordinary and frequent occasions, use this Manhattan chowder recipe, full of fresh vegetables.

    2 or more quarts clams (to get 1 pint chopped clams)
    1 cup water
    2 tablespoons vegetable oil
    1 clove garlic, minced
    1 stalk celery, with leaves, chopped
    1 onion, chopped
    1 cup diced potatoes
    4 large ripe tomatoes, peeled and chopped (or use canned ones)
    2 cups water
    ¼ teaspoon fresh or dried thyme, minced
    ½ teaspoon fresh or dried oregano, minced

Simmer clams in 1 cup water in large pot with lid until clams open fully, about 10 minutes. Remove clams; save juice. Remove meat and chop — should be about a pint. In a separate heavy pot, sauté garlic, onion, and celery in hot oil until soft. Add potatoes, tomatoes, and water. Bring to a simmer and cook gently, covered, until potatoes are soft. (Don't bring to a rolling boil as this tends to break down potatoes into crumbly bits.) Add reserved juice, clams, and herbs. Simmer another few minutes, maybe 5. (Don't overcook and toughen clams.) Season to taste and serve hot, for everyone.

Makes 8 or 9 cups.

Note: Instead of fresh clams and water for steaming, canned clams and bottled clam juice may be used. Same amounts — a pint (2 cups) of chopped clams and a cup of clam juice.

Creamed Scallop Treat

A creamy variation on a one-time restaurant favorite, Coquilles St.
Jacques. For all ages.

        4 cups chicken stock
        1 onion, cut up
        2 large potatoes, peeled and cut up
        1 teaspoon mace
        1 teaspoon thyme
        1 cup sea scallops, washed and cut in small pieces
        2 egg yolks
        1 cup whole milk or light cream

Add onion and potatoes to the stock and bring to a boil. Reduce heat
and simmer, covered, for 45 minutes. Purée in blender or food processor. Return to saucepan and reheat. In a small bowl, whisk the egg yolks
with the milk or cream, mace, and thyme. Add a little of the hot soup
to the egg mixture. Add a little more, whisking well. Then slowly add
the egg mix to the hot soup in the saucepan, stirring constantly. Cook
over very low heat until the soup begins to thicken. Quickly add the
scallops and continue cooking, stirring, over low heat until scallops are
barely done — about 4 to 5 minutes. Season to taste. Serve at once.

Makes about 8 cups.

Scallop and Broccoli Chowder

Scallops are good combined with anything, and they seem to stand up on their own, even when up against strong flavors. Most children like broccoli, especially chopped and hidden in the soup.

    3 slices of bacon
    2 medium onions, chopped
    1 sweet red pepper, seeded and chopped
    2 carrots, diced
    ¼ cup fresh parsley, minced
    2 cups broccoli florets, chopped
    4 ripe tomatoes, peeled and chopped
    2 cups diced potatoes
    1 cup clam juice (8-ounce bottle)
    2 cups chicken stock
    1 bay leaf, crumbled
    1 teaspoon soy sauce
    ½ teaspoon thyme
    1 ½ pounds sea scallops, washed, drained, and cut up

In a large pot, cook bacon until crisp and set aside. In drippings, sauté the onions, red pepper, carrots, and parsley until soft. Add remaining ingredients, except scallops, and simmer, covered, for 30 minutes. Add scallops and bacon, which has been crumbled. Simmer gently a few minutes, about 5, or until scallops are just done. Season to taste. Serve hot.

Makes almost 4 quarts.

Scallop and Eggplant Surprise

A surprisingly rewarding combination.

    1 small eggplant, peeled and cubed
    ½ cup water plus ½ cup boiling water
    1 pound sea scallops, washed, drained, and cut up
    2 tablespoons butter or margarine
    2 tablespoons flour
    2 cups milk, heated

Cook eggplant cubes in ½ cup water, covered, until they are soft. Put through blender or food processor to purée. Set aside. Cover the scallops with the ½ cup boiling water and simmer 3 to 4 minutes or until barely done. Set aside, with the liquid. Melt butter, add flour, and stir to make a roux. Gradually add 1 cup of the hot milk, stirring constantly, and cook over low heat until it slightly thickens. Add the scallops and liquid. Stir well. Blend in the eggplant purée. Stir in the remainder of hot milk and mix well. Simmer gently over very low heat to just get hot. Season to taste. Serve hot.

Makes about 8 cups.

Scallop and Snow-pea Chowder

First class. You'll need two soup pots, for big and little diners.

    4 tablespoons vegetable oil
    1 onion, finely chopped
    ½ cup mushrooms, chopped
    ½ sweet green pepper, seeded and chopped
    4 cups chicken stock
    1 cup diced peeled potatoes
    1 stalk celery, chopped
    1 teaspoon sage
    2 cups snow peas, fresh or frozen
    1 pound sea scallops, rinsed, drained, and cut up

Sauté onion, mushrooms, and green pepper in hot oil until vegetables are soft. Add stock, potatoes, celery, and sage. Divide into two cooking pots. In pot for adults, add half the snow peas. In pot for kids, chop up the snow peas first, then add to pot. Simmer both pots gently until vegetables are all tender. Divide scallops and add half to each pot; simmer for 4 to 5 minutes or until scallops are done. Season to taste. Serve hot.

Makes about 3 quarts.

Shrimp and Celery Supreme

There's no reason to give children a separate pot. They should like this as much as the adults will.

    2 tablespoons oil
    ½ cup celery leaves (tops), minced
    1 cup finely chopped celery stalk (bottoms)
    1 small onion, finely chopped
    2 tablespoons flour
    1 ½ cups whole milk, heated
    1 ½ cups chicken stock, heated
    1 packed cup shrimp, cooked, peeled, deveined, and cut in small
        pieces (2 small cans, 4 ½ ounces each, of shrimp, drained, may
        be used instead of fresh shrimp — not as good, but acceptable.)
    ¼ teaspoon mace
    dash of sherry (not enough to stun the kids)
    parsley for garnish (adults only)

Sauté celery leaves, celery, and onion in oil until celery is tender. Sprinkle on flour and mix well. Gradually add the hot chicken stock and the hot milk, stirring well, until slightly thickened and creamy. Stir in the shrimp, mace, and sherry. Season to taste and serve hot, garnished with parsley in cups/bowls for adults.

Makes about 6 cups.

Shrimp 'n Rice

There was a popular song back in the Forties that praised this combo: roughly, Shrimp and rice and everything nice; hold tight, hold tight, boogie racky-sacky want some seafood, Mama.

Catchy and silly, but that teenage generation liked it. All generations will like this soup.

   2 tablespoons oil, olive or vegetable
   2 medium onions, chopped
   1 sweet green pepper, seeded and chopped
   1 clove garlic, minced
   1 bay leaf, crumbled
   2 teaspoons paprika
   ¼ teaspoon mace
   ½ cup raw white rice
   2 large ripe tomatoes, peeled and chopped
   3 cups chicken stock
   1 pound shrimp, cooked, peeled, and deveined
   ½ cup whole milk or light cream
   1 tablespoon grated Parmesan cheese
   3 hard-cooked eggs, chopped

Sauté onions, pepper, and garlic in oil until soft. Stir in bay leaf, paprika, mace, rice, tomatoes, and chicken stock. Simmer gently for about 30 minutes or until rice is done. Add shrimp, milk, cheese, and eggs. Stir well. Season to taste. Serve hot.

Makes 3-plus quarts.

Southern Crab

Delicious, either side of the Mason-Dixon line, though not a soup I often have — crabs have become a very special treat!

I tried this with "fake crab," and it was surprisingly good. If you use it, cut the pieces into thin stringy short strips and mash them with a fork a bit to bring out the flavor.

1 small onion, minced
2 tablespoons vegetable oil or butter or margarine
2 tablespoons flour
3 cups milk, heated
1 ½ cups crab meat, picked over and flaked
2 egg yolks, hard cooked and grated
1 teaspoon Old Bay Seasoning
½ teaspoon Worcestershire sauce
¼ teaspoon paprika
¼ teaspoon mace
dash of sherry
parsley for garnish

In top of double boiler, over direct heat, sauté onion in hot oil (or butter), cooking until soft and golden. Stir in the flour to make a roux (paste). Gradually stir in the hot milk, stirring constantly, until slightly thickened. Stir in the remaining ingredients, except sherry and parsley. Place pan over boiling water in bottom of double boiler and heat thoroughly. Season to taste. Serve hot. Put a dash of sherry in bowls for adults and give them the parsley garnish as well.

Makes 5 or 6 cups.

In Charleston, She-Crab Soup is one of the specialties of the city. It's made from the female crab, using the meat and the crab roe, and has a more poignant flavor than soup from male crabs. I believe it also has become quite rare, but if you go there, be sure and try to locate some. The taste will be worth the effort.

Blue Fish and Rice

In late winter, I start to think about spring and summer and that usually leads to thoughts of fish and fishing. That's when I go to the fish market and see what could make a wonderful meal. There are so many good varieties of fish available year-round now, thanks to fish farms, and while I don't approve of the giant trawlers and nets that are taking too many of the ocean fish, I do occasionally get some of it. If you can find blue fish, this is a good recipe that all ages seem to like.

> 1 medium-size fillet of blue fish, about 1 pound, cut in small bite-size pieces
> 2 cups chicken stock
> 1 cup bottled clam juice
> 1 onion, sliced
> 1 stalk celery, cut up
> 1 slice lemon
> 4 or 5 cloves
> 2 sprigs parsley
> ¼ teaspoon peppercorns
> 1 bay leaf
> 3 tablespoons butter
> 3 tablespoons flour
> ½ cup whole milk (or more if desired)
> 1 cup cooked rice
> extra parsley for garnish, for adults

In a large pot, combine stock, clam juice, onion, celery, lemon, cloves, sprigs of parsley, peppercorns, and bay leaf. Bring to a boil, reduce heat, cover, and simmer for 45 minutes. Strain through a fine sieve or cheesecloth. Melt butter and stir in flour to make a roux. Gradually add the hot stock and cook, stirring constantly, until it slightly thickens. Add the pieces of blue fish and simmer until they flake, about 5 minutes. Add milk and the cooked rice. Season to taste. Heat and serve hot.

Makes 8 or 9 cups.

Tuna Bisque

Most kids like tuna fish in one form or another.

 Bones from a good-sized fish (get at a fish market)
 2 ½ cups water
 2 stalks celery, with leaves, 1 cut coarsely and 1 minced fine
 1 carrot, cut up
 3 tablespoons oil, vegetable or olive
 1 green pepper
 2 small onions, minced
 1 clove garlic, minced
 3 tablespoons flour
 ½ teaspoon thyme, fresh or dried
 1 pound boned and cubed fresh tuna (1 7-ounce can white tuna
  packed in water, drained and flaked, may be used — but it won't
  be as tasty as the real thing)
 1 cup whole milk
 ¼ cup capers, drained (optional)
 parsley for garnish

Combine fish bones, water, coarsely chopped celery, and carrot in a pot. Cover and simmer for about 30 minutes. Strain through a fine sieve, reserving liquid and discarding rest. (If you have been unable to get fish bones, use 2 ½ cups bland chicken stock instead of bones and water. By bland, I mean non-spicy.) Heat oil and sauté green pepper, onions, minced celery, and garlic until vegetables are soft. Sprinkle on flour and thyme and mix well. Slowly stir in the hot fish liquid and cook, stirring, over low heat to slightly thicken. Add the tuna and simmer gently, about 5 minutes, until fish flakes easily with a fork. Add milk. Season to taste. For little ones, hold the capers! This addition could be disastrous. But give a sprinkle of them to adults. Garnish with parsley, for adults.

Makes about 8 cups.

Note: Salmon or mackerel both work well in this recipe as substitutes for the tuna.

Vegetables

In the stark depth of winter, when icicles that can be measured in feet hang from the eaves and the snow banks form wide walls along the sides of my dirt road, my thoughts invariably turn to my garden. The catalogues of flowers and seeds have begun to arrive, and I find myself mesmerized and uplifted by the sights.

I sit by a sunny window where the strong low-riding winter sun slants easily inside, warming my shoulders and face, and I stare out to places where I know my garden sleeps, snugly buried beneath the thick blanket of snow. I look across the white lawn and past the visible top stones of the wall that stands guard over my sleeping perennial border; I look past the depression in the land and know the pond is firmly frozen, crisscrossed with paw prints of the dogs who have easily accepted its transformation from a swimming hole to a shortcut; I look across these familiar sights in my landscape and on to the field and, in my mind's eye, to the mowed path that leads to the summer garden and the rows of tender vegetables and cutting flowers — zinnias, cosmos, larkspur, marigolds, sweet peas climbing up sturdy lines of string, and low-growing calendulas meandering out of control. I look at this and can smell the sweet scents of the many colors and shapes of the flowers.

And I savor the vegetables to come. Lettuce and spinach for salads, basil and parsley for pesto, zucchini and little pale-golden summer squash, gathered when they are no longer than a small hand, juicy ripe red tomatoes, plump little yellow-plum tomatoes, green beans so tender they break in the picking, early peas for eating and freezing, crisp cucumbers, and sweet crunchy carrots. The old standbys. New things come and go every year, some staying awhile and replanted the following season, others given up as unsuitable or too difficult.

But always there are the rewards of growing things. As I look out the window, my days brighten. I will pick vegetables again. I will cut flowers. I will survive and even enjoy winter.

Creamy Artichoke

Every now and again, markets have wonderful buys on artichokes, though the cook shouldn't restrict her- or himself to those times. Frozen artichoke hearts are quite acceptable.

This soup is unusual and tasty and a different way to use artichokes. Strict vegetarians should substitute vegetable stock for chicken stock. Kids should like it.

6 artichokes, or 1 package frozen artichoke hearts
2 tablespoons vegetable oil
2 tablespoons flour
2 cups chicken stock, heated
2 teaspoons lemon juice
½ cup whole milk

Cook artichokes in water until tender; remove outer leaves (and eat in some marinade or with a dollop of mayo or yogurt.) Remove fuzzy tops from choke hearts and chop the hearts. If using frozen hearts, cook according to package directions, drain, and chop. Heat oil in saucepan and stir in flour to make a roux (paste); gradually add chicken stock, stirring until slightly thickened and creamy. Add the chopped hearts. Mix well. Cook over low heat for about five minutes. Purée in blender or food processor. Return to saucepan; add lemon juice and milk. Season to taste. Serve hot.

Makes about 1 quart.

Creamy Carrot

This is a pretty golden ocher color and disguises the fact of cooked carrots — kids nearly always like raw carrots, but scorn cooked ones.

    2 cups sliced carrots (or use frozen ones)
    2 cups beef stock
    ½ onion, sliced
    ½ teaspoon sugar
    ½ teaspoon thyme, fresh or dried
    1 tablespoon vegetable oil
    1 clove garlic
    1 tablespoon flour
    1 cup milk, heated

To the beef stock, add the carrots, onion, sugar, and thyme. Simmer until carrots are tender. Put in blender or food processor and purée. Set aside. In a saucepan, sauté the garlic in the oil. When golden brown, add the flour and mix well to make a paste. Gradually add the hot milk, stirring, until slightly thickened. Add the carrot and beef stock purée to the creamy mix in the saucepan and blend well. Season to taste. Serve hot.

Makes 5 cups.

Clear Eggplant

At first glance, this clear soup with soft "meaty" cubes floating in it would appear to be turtle, though few people serve turtle soup anymore. However, one taste and its own unique flavor stands out. An excellent choice before almost any main course.

    1 medium-sized eggplant
    2 tablespoons oil or butter or margarine
    2 tablespoons minced onion
    4 cups beef stock
    ¼ teaspoon Worcestershire sauce
    1 tablespoon sherry
    1 tablespoon apple juice

Peel and cube the eggplant. Reserve 1 cup of cubes, preferably from the small seedless end, and cover these with cold salted water. Set aside. Sauté onion in oil or butter until golden. Add cubed eggplant (except the reserved cup) and beef stock. Heat to boiling; reduce heat; cover; simmer for 40 to 45 minutes. Strain through a fine sieve or cheesecloth. Add the Worcestershire sauce. Divide soup into two pots, one for grown-ups and one for children. Drain the reserved eggplant cubes and add to the soup pot for big people. Reheat and simmer gently for about 10 minutes or until eggplant cubes are just soft. Add sherry. Add apple juice to pot for little ones. Reheat. Serve hot, with some cubes in each cup for adults.

Makes 7 or 8 cups.

Corn Chowder

For everyone. And easy.

> 2 tablespoons oil, vegetable or olive
> 1 onion
> ¼ teaspoon dry mustard
> 3 medium-sized potatoes, peeled and diced
> 1 cup water
> 2 cups corn, scraped from ears (or use canned corn niblets,
>   drained and mashed with a fork)
> 3 cups milk, heated
> ½ cup plain yogurt

In a large saucepan, heat oil and sauté onion until golden. Stir in mustard. Add potatoes and water. Simmer until potatoes are soft. Add corn and hot milk. Cook over very low heat until corn softens. Add yogurt. Season to taste and serve hot.

Makes 2-plus quarts.

This soup works as a vegetarian entree. For a complete meal, serve it with a green salad and creamy dressing, such as Russian or blue cheese, and a dense grain bread or dark pumpernickel. Cheesecake is good for dessert with this meal.

Creamed Onion

If you like onions and creamed onions, you'll like this. The creamy aspect makes it acceptable to kids. I especially like to make this in the late spring and early summer when the sweet Vidalia onions have arrived from Georgia. (A Vidalia grown in any other state is a Vidalia-type onion. A true Vidalia can only come from a certain region in Georgia that is licensed by the state to grow these unique onions.)

> 3 or 4 large sweet onions, thinly sliced in half-rings or
>   quarter rings
> 4 tablespoons oil or butter or margarine
> 3 tablespoons flour
> ½ teaspoon salt
> 1 ½ cups chicken stock, heated
> 1 ½ cups milk, heated (heat the 2 liquids together)
> ½ teaspoon Worcestershire sauce
> ½ teaspoon mace

Heat the milk and stock together and keep hot in saucepan. In a large skillet, sauté the separated onion rings in the oil until they are soft and golden. Sprinkle on the flour and salt and mix well. Add a little of the hot stock mix to the skillet and stir to thicken. When creamy, add the onion mix to the hot liquids in the saucepan. Cook over very low heat, stirring, until it slightly thickens. Add the Worcestershire and mace. Season to taste. Cook gently for about 15 minutes. Serve hot.

Makes 5 or 6 cups.

Cuke and Potato

A year-round favorite with us, especially in winter.

    2 cups peeled, seeded, and diced cucumbers
    ½ cup white part of leeks, thinly sliced
    1 cup diced peeled potatoes
    ¼ cup minced parsley
    2 tablespoons oil
    2 ½ cups chicken stock
    ½ teaspoon dry mustard
    ½ teaspoon summer savory or marjoram, (if fresh, mince)
    ¼ teaspoon white pepper
    ½ cup commercial sour cream
    more parsley for garnish for adults

Sauté cucumbers, leeks, potatoes and parsley in hot oil over low heat until vegetables are soft. Stir in mustard. Add chicken stock, cover, and simmer gently for about 15 minutes. Add savory or marjoram, pepper, and sour cream. Mix well. Season to taste and serve hot, garnished with parsley for adults.

                                        Makes 6 or 7 cups.

Curried Creamy Green Pea

Easy and tasty and not too much curry flavor to turn off kids.

1 cup frozen green peas
1 small onion, chopped
1 medium carrot, diced
1 medium-sized potato, peeled and diced
1 stalk celery, with leaves, chopped
1 clove garlic, minced
1 cup chicken stock
1 tablespoon vegetable oil
1 tablespoon flour
2 teaspoons curry powder
1 cup milk, heated

Combine peas, onion, carrot, potato, celery, garlic, and chicken stock in a large saucepan. Bring to simmer, cover, and cook gently for 30 to 40 minutes. Purée all in blender or food processor. Heat oil; add flour and curry powder; stir to make a roux (paste). Gradually add hot milk, stirring constantly, and cook until creamy and slightly thickened. Mix well with the vegetable purée; simmer together briefly. Season to taste and serve hot.

Makes 5 or 6 cups.

Note: If you have any leftover soup, mix it with some V-8 juice and heat. Delicious.

Eggplant Espinaca

Espinaca is spinach in Spanish. Leave it at that and let the little ones guess. This recipe makes a lot. Cut in half or freeze any leftovers. We usually have this soon after Thanksgiving, as a change from leftover turkey and stuffing.

2 cloves garlic, minced
2 tablespoons oil, olive or vegetable
1 large sweet Spanish onion
1 medium eggplant, diced (do not peel)
1 box frozen chopped spinach, thawed
1 large can crushed tomatoes
6 to 8 cups chicken (or turkey) stock
1 teaspoon oregano
cooked pasta

Sauté garlic and onion in oil until golden. Add eggplant and cook until just soft. Add remaining ingredients. Simmer gently, covered, for about 45 minutes. Season to taste, serve hot over cooked pasta, such as ziti, rigatoni, spirals, etc., in the bottom of the soup plate.

Makes almost 4 quarts.

Creamy Fennel

Fennel has such a wonderful flavor, with that delicate hint of licorice, something that children like. (It's also good as a vegetable, julienned and simply boiled, then tossed in butter or margarine with a tad of salt.)

2 or 3 fennel stalks, (tops removed), diced
2 tablespoons butter or margarine
1 large sweet onion, diced
1 teaspoon marjoram
1 cup beef stock
2 tablespoons flour
1 cup whole milk
½ cup light sour cream

Melt the butter and add the fennel and onion. Sauté gently until vegetables begin to get soft. Stir in marjoram and a ½ cup of the beef stock. Simmer for about 10 minutes or until vegetables are quite soft. Mix the flour with a little of the milk to make a smooth paste. Stir into the vegetables and mix well. Stir in remaining stock and milk. Cook over low heat, stirring, until it thickens. Add the sour cream and continue cooking until it is good and hot. (Add a little sherry to cups for adults if desired.) Serve hot.

Makes 1 quart.

Green Beans and Bacon

A good combination.

    2 slices bacon

    2 cups finely cut green beans, fresh or frozen

    ½ onion

    2 tablespoons flour

    2 cups chicken stock, heated

    ½ cup whole milk

    ½ teaspoon parsley, minced

    pinch of nutmeg

Cook bacon until crisp in a saucepan. Drain, reserving 2 tablespoons fat. Crumble bacon and set aside. Return reserved fat to saucepan. Add onion and beans and sauté over low heat for about 10 or 12 minutes or until beans are tender, stirring to cook evenly. Sprinkle on flour and stir well. Gradually add the hot stock, stirring, until slightly thickened. Add milk, parsley, nutmeg, and crumbled bacon. Heat and serve hot.

Makes 1 quart, maybe more.

Cucumber Surprise

If I have an abundant supply of cucumbers in my garden in the summer, I peel them and slice them into long strips and freeze them on a cookie sheet. When they are frozen, I package them in freezer bags and use them all winter in soups or sautéed in a little oil with salt and pepper as a vegetable.

These ingredients may sound weird, but don't knock them until you've tried this soup.

> 1 onion, chopped
> 2 tablespoons vegetable oil or butter or margarine
> 2 large cucumbers, peeled, large seeds scooped out, chopped
> 2 cups chicken stock
> ½ teaspoon prepared horseradish
> ½ cup peanuts, preferably unsalted
> 1 cup whole milk
> ½ teaspoon fresh cilantro, minced
> toasted croutons for garnish

In a large pot, sauté the onions in oil until golden. Add the cucumbers, stock, and horseradish. Bring to a boil, reduce heat, cover, and simmer about 30 minutes. Meanwhile, purée peanuts in milk in blender or food processor. After cucumbers are cooked, add the peanut milk and cilantro and reheat just to simmering. Season to taste. Serve hot, with a handful of hot toasted croutons for all ages. (If you want to be on the really safe side, reserve the cilantro and use it as a second garnish for adults. It has a strong flavor, but as this is such a small amount it should be acceptable to everyone.)

Makes about 6 cups.

Leek and Potato

Creamy and lightly flavored. This is good with onion or garlic
breadsticks. Or try spreading oil and grated Parmesan cheese on Rye
Krisps and toasting them, then cool slightly to recrisp and firm up
again and serve with the soup.

     2 large leeks, white bottoms and a little of the green top
     1 medium onion, chopped
     2 medium potatoes, peeled and cubed
     ½ teaspoon salt
     3 tablespoons oil, vegetable or olive
     1 tablespoon flour
     ½ teaspoon thyme
     2 cups chicken stock, heated
     ½ cup whole milk
     minced chives for garnish for adults

Heat oil in a wide saucepan or deep skillet and add leeks, onion, and
potatoes. Sprinkle with salt. Cover and cook gently over low heat until
vegetables are soft. Sprinkle on flour and mix well. Stir in thyme.
Gradually add the hot stock, stirring, and cook until a little creamy in
texture. Add milk. Season to taste and garnish with chives for adults.
Makes about 2 quarts.

Mushroom-Vegetable

Years ago I had to wait for summer to serve this. Now, with the excellent fresh vegetables available in markets, it has become a year-round meal. It's light and thoroughly satisfying and liked by all.

> ¼ cup oil, olive or vegetable
> 2 sweet green peppers, seeded and chopped
> 2 medium-sized zucchinis, chopped (do not peel)
> 1 pound mushrooms, chopped
> 1 medium onion, chopped
> 1 clove garlic, minced
> 1 ½ cups canned chopped tomatoes (if using fresh ripe ones, use 4 large ones)
> ½ teaspoon thyme
> 1 cup tomato juice
> 1 cup chicken stock
> hot cooked rice

Sauté peppers, zucchinis, mushrooms, onion, and garlic in oil over low heat until just soft. Add tomatoes, thyme, tomato juice, and chicken stock. Bring to a boil, reduce heat, cover, and simmer for 20 to 30 minutes. Season to taste. Serve hot, over hot cooked rice.

Makes 2 quarts.

Parsleyed Potato

You have to finely mince the parsley to get kids to eat this soup. Don't leave any whole curly leaves floating around!

  3 tablespoons vegetable oil
  2 tablespoons onion, minced
  1 clove garlic, minced
  2 medium potatoes, peeled and diced
  ½ teaspoon salt
  1 tablespoon hot water
  4 cups parsley, finely minced
  2 tablespoons flour
  2 cups chicken stock, heated
  ½ cup plain yogurt
  freshly ground black pepper, for adults

Sauté onion and garlic in oil over low heat until soft. Add potato, salt, and hot water and cover pan. Over very low heat, let steam until potatoes are tender, but not mushy. Add parsley and mix in. Sprinkle on flour and mix well. Gradually add the hot chicken stock, stirring and simmering, until slightly thickened. Add yogurt. Heat. Serve hot with some freshly ground black pepper for adults.

Makes 2 quarts.

Parsnip Ginger

Another unusual and delicious combo, and nothing that should be offensive to any young age. The parsnip/celery/ginger flavors blend beautifully.

    2 tablespoons vegetable oil
    2 medium parsnips, scraped and diced
    2 stalks celery, with leaves, chopped
    1 onion, chopped
    1 clove garlic, minced
    2 tablespoons flour
    2 teaspoons ground or finely minced fresh ginger
    ½ teaspoon ground cumin seed
    ¼ teaspoon chili powder
    ½ teaspoon celery seed
    4 cups chicken stock, heated
    ½ cup whole milk

In a large saucepan with a tightly fitting cover, over very low heat, sauté parsnips, celery, onion, and garlic in butter until just soft. Sprinkle on flour, ginger, spices, and celery seed and stir well. Gradually add the hot stock and cook, stirring until well blended and slightly thickened. Add the milk. Cook gently for a few minutes, about 3 or 4. Season to taste and serve hot.

Makes about 2 quarts.

Party Parsnip

Elegant and easy.

> 3 or 4 medium-sized parsnips
> water
> 1 tablespoon oil
> 1 tablespoon flour
> ¼ teaspoon ground allspice
> 2 cups beef stock, heated
> ½ cup whole milk
> touch of sherry
> parsley for garnish, for adults

Scrape parsnips with vegetable scraper and cut in chunks. Boil in water to cover until soft. Drain, saving some of the water. Purée in blender or food processor with about ¼ cup cooking water. In a saucepan, heat oil and add flour to make a roux (paste). Add allspice. Gradually stir in the hot beef stock, stirring, until just slightly thickened, about the consistency of half-and-half cream. This should not be too thick; if it is, add a little of the cooking water to thin. Add the parsnip purée, milk, and a touch of sherry. Serve hot, with parsley for garnish, for adults.

Makes 5 or 6 cups.

Paul's Pea Soup

I never met Paul, but this recipe was given to me by a friend who said "This is Paul's recipe, and you know what a great cook he is." He is.

   1 tablespoon butter or margarine
   2 tablespoons oil, olive or vegetable
   1 onion, finely chopped
   1 clove garlic, minced and crushed
   2 cups fresh peas (or use 1 package frozen)
   1 teaspoon curry powder
   2 tablespoons flour
   2 cups chicken stock, heated
   ¾ cup whole milk
   ½ cup cooked chicken, shredded of finely chopped

In a saucepan, heat oil and butter, and sauté onion and garlic for 3 minutes. Add the peas, cover, and cook over very low heat until they are soft. Stir in curry powder. Remove from heat, sprinkle on flour and mix well; blend in the hot stock. Return to heat and bring to simmering, stirring constantly. Simmer 1 minute. Purée in blender or food processor. Reheat with milk and cooked chicken. Season to taste. Serve hot.

Makes 6 cups.

Potato Cream

The flavor will remind children of mashed potatoes and will be a hit.
The "cream" is in the name only.

> 2 cups peeled and cut-up potatoes, about 3 medium ones
> 1 cup chicken stock
> 1 onion, chopped
> 1 clove garlic, minced
> 1 tablespoon vegetable oil
> 1 cup whole milk, heated
> 1 tablespoon fresh cilantro, chopped

Put potatoes and chicken stock in a saucepan and cook, covered, over
low heat until potatoes are soft. Meanwhile, sauté onion and garlic in
oil until golden. When potatoes are cooked, mix them with the onion
and garlic and purée all together, in blender or food processor. Return to
saucepan and add milk. Heat through. (If too thick, add more milk.)
Garnish with fresh cilantro for adults only.

Makes about 5 cups.

Red-Red Soup

Beets and tomatoes, wonderful colors. Tasty too.

> 4 or 5 large beets, tops and tails removed, scrubbed and quartered
> water
> 1 clove garlic, minced
> 1 medium onion, minced
> 4 or 5 ripe tomatoes, or use canned ones, finely chopped
> 2 tablespoons oil, vegetable or olive
> ½ cup rich beef stock or canned consomme
> sour cream for garnish

Cook beets in water to cover until tender. Remove and peel. Set aside. (Canned ones may be used instead.) Sauté garlic and onion in oil until golden brown. Add tomatoes and cook for about 3 minutes. Put beets and tomatoes, onion, and garlic in food processor and mince until beets are finely chopped but not puréed. You want some texture. Return to pan and add beef stock. Heat. If too thick, add a little more stock. Serve with a small dollop of sour cream on top of soup in bowls. It's up to you, and the younger sest, whether they'll want this or not. Serve hot.

Makes about 7 or 8 cups.

Red Rice

Do not add the rice until you are ready to serve this — it will get too soft. The rest of the soup can be kept hot and waiting for a long time.

  2 tablespoons oil, olive or vegetable
  1 onion, minced
  1 stalk celery, with leaves, minced
  1 green pepper, seeded and minced
  6 ripe tomatoes, peeled and chopped (or use canned ones)
  2 cups chicken stock
  ¼ teaspoon ground cloves
  ¼ teaspoon paprika
  ½ teaspoon basil
  1 teaspoon parsley
  1 cup hot cooked rice

Sauté onion, celery, and pepper, in oil until soft. Add the remaining ingredients, except the rice. Bring to a boil, stirring, reduce heat, cover, and simmer for 30 to 40 minutes. Add rice just before serving. Season to taste. Serve hot.

Makes 7 or 8 cups.

Sassy Asparagus

Depending on where you live, fresh asparagus may or may not be available when you want to make this. If it's not, use frozen. (I've even resorted to canned asparagus and had this come out okay. If you do that, use a 10 ½-ounce can green asparagus, with the liquid.)

        2 cups fresh or frozen asparagus, cut in pieces
        water for cooking
        2 tablespoons vegetable oil
        2 tablespoons flour
        1 cup chicken stock, heated
        1 cup whole milk
        ½ cup orange juice

Barely cover asparagus pieces with boiling water and cook until just tender. Drain, reserving the liquid and a few tips for garnish. Purée remainder in blender or food processor. Heat oil, stir in flour to make a roux (paste) and gradually add about 1 cup of the hot asparagus liquid and the hot chicken stock, stirring until slightly thickened. Add asparagus purée. Stir in the milk and orange juice. Heat gently. Serve hot. Garnish with a reserved tip or two in cups for adults.

Makes 1 quart.

Simple Green Lima

My children would never eat lima beans as a vegetable, but they would eat this soup made with them — so long as I didn't call it by its real name.

 2 tablespoons vegetable oil
 1 small sweet onion, chopped
 2 cups lima beans, fresh or frozen
 2 cups chicken stock
 2 tablespoons chopped fresh parsley
 1 teaspoon fresh or dried oregano
 ¼ cup light sour cream
 ¼ cup plain yogurt
 1 tablespoon honey

Heat oil in a large saucepan and sauté onion until soft. Add lima beans, chicken stock, parsley, and oregano. Simmer until beans are soft. Purée in blender or food processor. Return to saucepan and heat. Stir in sour cream, yogurt, and honey. Season to taste. Heat. Serve hot.

Makes 1 quart.

Sprout Delight

Another instance where it's better not to say the whole name. Brussels sprouts are apt to be an acquired taste. Any kids who like cabbage will like them, and those who've had this soup all liked it.

2 tablespoons oil or butter or margarine
1 onion, chopped
2 tablespoons flour
1 ½ cups buttermilk, heated
2 cups fresh Brussels sprouts (or use 1 package frozen)
1 cup beef stock
1 teaspoon paprika
¼ teaspoon ground allspice
½ teaspoon mace

In the oil or butter, sauté the onion until golden. Sprinkle on the flour and mix well. Stir in the hot buttermilk to make a cream sauce, stirring constantly, until it thickens. Remove from heat. Meanwhile, cook the sprouts in the beef stock until they are tender. Combine them with the cream sauce. Put through blender or food processor to purée. Return to saucepan. Add the paprika, allspice, and mace. Stir well. Season to taste. Heat thoroughly, but do not boil. Serve hot. (If too thick, add more buttermilk or a little whole milk.)

Makes about 5 cups.

Sweet Onion Brown

Be sure to slice and chop the onions very thin to make this a hit with little ones. Big chunks of onion in the soup are almost guaranteed to be rejects.

    4 large sweet onions (Vidalia or Spanish are excellent)
    1 clove garlic, minced
    2 tablespoons oil, vegetable or olive
    ½ teaspoon salt
    1 teaspoon cornstarch
    1 quart rich beef stock (or use canned consomme)
    slices of toasted French bread
    grated fresh Parmesan cheese (or use dried if necessary)

Thinly slice and chop up the onions. Stir them into the oil with the garlic and salt in a large saucepan that has a cover. Sauté over very low heat, covered, for 20 to 30 minutes or until lightly browned. Mix cornstarch with about a ½ cup of beef stock, then add this and the remaining stock to the onions. Mix well. Bring to simmer, stirring, to blend in cornstarch and slightly thicken. Be sure nothing has stuck to bottom of pan. Simmer another 20 to 30 minutes. Season to taste.

Makes 1 ½ quarts.

Serve hot, poured over a slice of toasted French bread in the bottom of the soup plate. Serve with a generous sprinkle of grated cheese on top of soup. Big hit.

Turnip Bottom

Another gently flavored creamy puréed soup that kids will like because they probably won't know what it is. Don't use yellow turnips for this — they have a stronger flavor.

    4 medium-sized white (purple-topped) turnips, nubby
        tops removed
    1 onion, chopped
    2 tablespoons butter or margarine
    ½ teaspoon salt
    ½ cup water
    1 cup chicken or rich vegetable stock
    1 cup whole milk
    ½ teaspoon fresh basil (or dried if unable to get fresh), minced
        parsley for garnish

Slice and chop turnips. In a good-sized saucepan, combine turnips, onion, butter, salt, and water. Cover tightly and simmer over very low heat for about 30 minutes or until turnips are soft. Purée in blender or food processor. Return to saucepan. To the turnip purée, stir in the chicken stock, milk, and basil. Heat. Season to taste. Serve hot with parsley for garnish, for adults.

Makes about 6 cups.

In the South where I grew up, we only ate the greens of the turnips and gave the root part to a farmer to feed to his pigs. I was in college before I realized these delicious bottoms were also for human consumption. Lucky pigs.

Vegetable with Barley

Simple and delicious. For a big meal, serve it over hot cooked rice.

    some beef bones
    1 cup dried barley
    3 quarts water
    2 medium white or yellow turnips, peeled and finely diced
    2 carrots, diced
    1 sweet green pepper, seeded and finely chopped
    3 to 4 small onions, finely chopped
    1 clove garlic, minced
    1 tablespoon tomato paste
    1 heaping tablespoon prepared yellow mustard
    2 teaspoons oregano
    ¼ cup dry cocktail sherry or white wine
    ¼ cup apple juice

In a large pot, combine bones, barley, water, turnips, carrots, pepper, onions, garlic, and tomato paste. Bring to a boil, reduce heat, cover, and simmer for 1 ½ hours. Remove bones. Stir in mustard and oregano. Divide soup into two pots. Add sherry or wine to pot for grown-ups; add apple juice to pot for kids. Simmer briefly. Serve hot.

Makes 3 or 4 quarts.

Vegetable Oriental

This is a nice mix of vegetables and a dab of fruit. It should appeal to adults and children. Cut in half for smaller amount.

8 cups beef stock, homemade or canned
1 teaspoon each of parsley, crumbled bay leaves, and thyme
1 onion, chopped
1 sweet green pepper, seeded and chopped
1 small hot green pepper, as jalapeño, minced
1 clove garlic, minced
2 tablespoons oil, olive or vegetable
1 tablespoon cornstarch
½ cup cold water
4 to 5 large ripe tomatoes, peeled and chopped (or canned ones)
3 medium carrots, sliced
3 stalks celery, with leaves, chopped
1 fennel bulb, chopped
1 teaspoon ground ginger
½ teaspoon ground cloves
1 tablespoon soy sauce
½ teaspoon caraway seeds
1 tablespoon vinegar
1 tablespoon molasses
½ cup pearl barley
1 small can pineapple chunks, cut in very thin strips, with juice
½ cup bean sprouts, cut into little amounts
2 tablespoons sherry

In a large heavy pot, sauté onions, sweet and hot peppers, and garlic in oil until soft. Combine cornstarch and water and blend well. Add some of the hot stock to this and mix well. Add cornstarch mix and the rest of the hot beef stock to the pot with the sautéed vegetables. Add tomatoes, carrots, celery, fennel, ginger, cloves, soy sauce, caraway seeds, vinegar, molasses, and barley. Mix well. Bring to simmering and cook over low heat for an hour or so. Add pineapple, bean sprouts, and sherry. Season to taste. Cook for another 10 or 15 minutes. Serve hot.

Makes a lot, more than 4 quarts.

Winter Pink Squash

Any of the winter squashes will work in this recipe — acorn, butternut, or others.

    1 winter squash (or use 2 cups frozen winter squash)
    1 tablespoon oil
    1 tablespoon flour
    1 cup beef stock, heated
    ½ cup milk
    ½ cup tomato juice
    1 teaspoon mace
    1 tablespoon paprika

Split squash down middle and place in a shallow pan, cut side down, with about a cup of water. Cover with foil and bake in a 350-degree oven until soft, about 30 to 40 minutes, depending on size of squash. When soft, scoop out seeds and pulpy matter and discard. Either peel squash or scoop out flesh. Purée flesh in blender or food processor or mash until smooth. Use 2 cups puréed squash for soup recipe.

Heat oil and stir in flour to make a roux (paste); gradually stir in hot stock, stirring, and cook until it thickens slightly. Stir in squash, milk, tomato juice, mace, and paprika. Serve hot.

Makes 1 quart.

Winter Vegetable

This recipe was given to me a long time ago, when I was first learning to cook. It's still a favorite, and it's easy.

>   2 pounds beef, cubed
>   1 large can plum tomatoes
>   2 to 3 onions, chopped
>   ½ pound mushrooms, chopped
>   2 stalks celery, with leaves, chopped
>   ½ teaspoon thyme
>   ½ teaspoon basil
>   ½ teaspoon marjoram
>   1 teaspoon parsley
>   1 tablespoon Worcestershire sauce
>   1 teaspoon salt
>   water to barely cover
>   1 package frozen chopped broccoli (or chopped spinach)
>   1 package frozen mixed vegetables

In a large pot, combine beef, tomatoes, onions, mushrooms, celery, herbs, Worcestershire sauce, and salt. Cover with water. Bring to simmering, cover, and cook over low heat for 2 hours or more or until meat is very tender. Add frozen vegetables. Return to simmering and cook gently for another ½ hour. Season to taste. Serve hot.

Makes a lot, about 4 quarts.

Zucchini-Tomato Medley

This should appeal to all ages.

    2 tablespoons vegetable oil

    1 onion, chopped

    ½ sweet red pepper, seeded and chopped

    1 clove garlic, minced

    2 medium-sized zucchinis, chopped

    4 large ripe tomatoes, peeled and chopped (or use canned ones)

    1 teaspoon oregano, fresh or dried

    1 tablespoon flour

    2 cups chicken stock, heated

    pimientos as garnish for adults (maybe little ones too)

Sauté onion, red pepper, and garlic in oil until soft. Stir in zucchini, tomatoes and oregano. Sprinkle on flour and mix well. Gradually add the hot stock, stirring, and cook until slightly thickened. Cover and simmer over low heat about 30 minutes. Season to taste. Cut pimientos into tiny strips and use as a garnish. Serve hot.

Makes more than 2 quarts.

This is good over hot cooked rice or pasta as a bigger meal.

Fruit

As any child knows, fruit is something to be peeled and eaten plain or cut up on cereal. Even though the idea of soups with fruits may well be enticing to the cook and to grown-ups, you might be taking a chance on having it eaten by little ones if you mention the word fruit. Therefore, as an alternate, I might suggest the acronym TOPs, for tomato, orange, and pumpkin (you will notice that I consider tomatoes to be fruits as well as vegetables.) TOP soups are something any respectable grown-up or child would gladly eat. Certainly don't call these Surprise Soups! Children like surprises wrapped in pretty paper and tied with a ribbon, not floating in a soup bowl.

Avocado Green

An ambiguous title that should be intriguing to adults and children. This is good served in small amounts as a first course.

  1 ripe avocado
  1 tablespoon fresh parsley
  1 tablespoon oil, vegetable or olive
  1 tablespoon flour
  1 ½ cups chicken stock, heated
  ¼ cup whole milk
  ¼ cup lime juice
  pinch of chili powder (about ⅛ teaspoon)
  pinch of white pepper
  chopped chives or more parsley for garnish, for adults

Scoop out avocado and purée with parsley in blender or food processor. Heat oil and add flour to make a roux (paste); gradually add the hot chicken stock, stirring, to slightly thicken. Cook over very low heat, stirring, 3 or 4 minutes. Add avocado and parsley purée. Blend thoroughly. Stir in milk, lime juice, chili powder, and white pepper. Season to taste. Serve hot, with the garnish for adults only.

Makes about 3 cups.

Chicken Orange

I call this Souper! I originally used light cream in this recipe, but now have changed to whole milk. Use whichever you prefer, depending on how daring you are. All ages will go for this. It makes an elegant meal, especially served with a green salad and some hot buttered rolls. I've used it for small Sunday-lunch parties.

1 small chicken, 2 to 2 ½ pounds, cut in pieces
about 1 ½ quarts water (to cover chicken pieces)
1 ½ teaspoons ground ginger
1 teaspoon soy sauce
½ teaspoon salt
1 tablespoon honey
1 tablespoon vinegar
1 tablespoon parsley, minced
2 tablespoons vegetable oil
1 onion, chopped
1 orange — the rind, finely chopped; the flesh, seeded and chopped
2 tablespoons flour
1 ½ cups orange juice
1 small can (8 ounces) tomato sauce
½ cup whole milk (or light cream)
hot cooked rice.

Put chicken pieces in large saucepan with water. Add ginger, soy sauce, salt, honey, vinegar, and parsley. Bring to a boil, reduce heat, cover, and simmer for 1 hour. Remove chicken pieces. Remove skin and bones and discard (actually, I pitch the bones, but save the skin for the dogs). Cut meat into small pieces and set aside. Skim off any fat from liquid. In a skillet, heat oil; slowly sauté the onion and chopped orange rind until they are soft and golden. Sprinkle on the flour and mix well. Add the orange juice and tomato sauce and cook, stirring constantly, until slightly thickened. Blend this orange sauce into the chicken stock in the saucepan. Add the chicken meat, the chopped orange flesh, and the milk. Season to taste. Serve hot over some hot cooked rice in each bowl.

Makes 2 to 3 quarts.

Creamy Tomato Treat

Lovely.

    2 tablespoons oil or butter or margarine
    1 onion, chopped
    1 carrot, diced
    1 stalk celery, with leaves, diced
    2 tablespoons flour
    ½ teaspoon chili powder
    ½ teaspoon ground savory
    2 cups chicken stock, heated
    4 large ripe tomatoes, (or use canned ones,) peeled and chopped
    thin lemon slices for garnish, for adults

Heat oil or butter and add onion, carrot, and celery. Sauté over low heat until soft. Sprinkle on the flour and stir well. Stir in chili powder and savory. Gradually add the hot stock, stirring, and cook until slightly thickened. Add the tomatoes. Purée all, except lemon, in blender or food processor. Season. Reheat. Serve hot with lemon slices for garnish for adults.

Makes about 6 cups.

Halloween Pumpkin

Halloween is in the fall and this book is about winter soups, but I'm taking a little leeway here. Canned pumpkin is readily available anytime, anywhere.

After Halloween, I cook my pumpkins and freeze the flesh to use during the winter months. So even though I make the soup in winter, the product is really from Halloween — hence the name.

2 cups puréed pumpkin, fresh-cooked or canned
1 tablespoon vegetable oil
1 small onion
1 clove garlic, minced
1 tablespoon flour
1 ½ cups milk, heated
1 teaspoon brown sugar
pinch (about ⅛ teaspoon) ground cloves
¼ cup sherry
¼ cup apple juice
light sour cream for garnish

Heat oil in saucepan and add onion and garlic; sauté until golden and soft. Stir in flour to make a roux (paste); gradually add the hot milk, stirring constantly, and cook gently until slightly thickened. Put pumpkin purée, milk mixture, sugar, and cloves in blender or food processor and blend until creamy and smooth. Divide into two saucepans. Add sherry to pot for adults, apple juice to pot for kids. Heat. Serve with a small dollop of sour cream as a garnish, for grown-ups and maybe for kids.

Makes 4 to 5 cups.

Hawaiian Hot Pot

This is a crazy mixture of fruits and vegetables, with a sweet-and-sour overtone. Good.

2 tablespoons oil
1 clove garlic, minced
1 small onion, chopped
½ sweet green pepper, seeded and chopped
1 sweet red pepper, seeded and chopped
1 cucumber peeled, seeded, and chopped
1 stalk celery, with leaves, chopped
1 cup chopped cabbage
1 large firm apple, such as a Granny Smith, peeled, cored,
   and chopped
1 teaspoon ground ginger
3 tablespoons vinegar
¼ cup packed brown sugar
¼ cup canned crushed pineapple
3 cups beef stock or canned beef broth
1 cup apple juice
½ cup grapefruit juice
hot cooked rice

Heat oil and sauté garlic, onion, green pepper, and red pepper until vegetables are soft. Add remaining ingredients, except cooked rice. Bring to boiling, reduce heat, cover, and simmer until cabbage and celery are tender. Serve over hot cooked rice in bottom of bowls. Delicious.

Makes 2-plus quarts.

Lemon-Dill

This has a nice snappy taste and should be liked by all ages. I find that kids like tart tastes, such as old-fashioned lemon drops that have less sugar than modern ones.

> 1 tablespoon oil or butter or margarine
> 1 clove garlic, minced
> 1 onion, chopped
> ½ lemon, sliced
> 2 cups chicken stock
> 1 potato, peeled and cut up
> little grated lemon rind plus 2 tablespoons lemon juice (the other half of the lemon)
> 1 teaspoon sugar
> 2 tablespoons fresh dill weed, minced
> 1 cup whole milk

In a large saucepan, sauté garlic and onion in oil until soft and golden. Add sliced lemon and chicken stock. Bring to a boil, reduce heat, cover, and simmer for 30 minutes. Strain through a sieve. To lemony stock, add the potato and return to a boil. Reduce heat, cover, and simmer for 15 minutes or until potato is soft. Purée in blender or food processor. Return to saucepan and add grated lemon rind and juice, sugar, dill weed, and milk. Heat just to simmering. Season to taste. Serve hot.

Makes 4 to 5 cups.

Orange Choice

Nice color and tasty. This has a smooth creamy texture.

> 2 tablespoons oil, vegetable or olive
> 2 medium onions, chopped
> 1 orange with peel, cut up in small pieces
> 1 clove garlic, minced
> 2 tablespoons flour
> 2 cups beef stock, heated
> ¾ cup orange juice
> ½ cup whole milk
> sherry, for adults

In a covered saucepan, slowly sauté the orange, onions, and garlic in oil until onions are golden and translucent and orange is slightly browned — keeping the lid on will prevent evaporation of juices. Uncover and sprinkle on flour; mix well. Gradually add the hot stock, stirring, and cook until slightly thickened. Add orange juice and milk. Heat. Strain soup though a sieve. Reheat. Serve hot, with a little sherry in cups for adults.

Makes 1 quart.

Party Apple Parsnip

As parsnips are so easy to find in markets, I never bother to grow them in my vegetable garden and freeze as I do with so many vegetables. I love them in soups or simply cooked and served with butter as a vegetable. Their delicate slightly sweet flavor is liked by all ages.

4 medium-sized parsnips, scraped and diced
2 carrots, diced
2 tart firm apples, peeled, cored, and diced
3 tablespoons vegetable oil
1 teaspoon ground ginger
4 cups chicken stock, heated
2 heaping tablespoons plain yogurt
any minced fresh herb for garnish, for grown-ups (oregano or parsley are recommended)

Sauté parsnips, carrots, and apples in oil until a little soft. Sprinkle on flour and ginger and mix well. Gradually add the hot chicken stock and cook, stirring, over very low heat for a few minutes, about 5 to 7 minutes or until slightly thickened and vegetables are completely soft. Blend in the yogurt. Season to taste, heat, and serve hot, with fresh herb garnish for adults.

Makes about 2 ½ quarts.

Pumpkin Eater Purée

For Peter and anyone else.

1 cup potatoes, peeled and cubed
4 cups chicken stock
2 tablespoons vegetable oil
2 tablespoons diced onion
1 tablespoon flour
½ cup whole milk, heated
1 cup cooked pumpkin
½ cup finely diced carrot
½ cup finely chopped celery stalk

Cook potatoes in stock until soft and set aside. In 1 tablespoon oil (save 1), sauté onion until golden. Sprinkle on flour and mix well. Stir in milk and cook over very low heat until slightly thickened. Put potatoes and stock, onion-milk mix, and cooked pumpkin through blender or food processor to purée. Return to saucepan and set aside. In remaining tablespoon oil, sauté carrots and celery until barely cooked, still a little crunchy. Combine everything. Heat and serve hot.

Makes 2-plus quarts.

Tomato Creole

This is when the tomato is the main fruit.

1 large can (1 pound 10 ounces) whole tomatoes

½ cup apple juice

2 stalks celery, with leaves, cup up

½ large sweet green pepper, seeded and cup up

1 small hot green pepper, such as jalapeño, cup up, seeds and all

½ onion, sliced

½ teaspoon crushed bay leaves

1 tablespoon fresh parsley

1 teaspoon lemon juice

1 teaspoon sugar

dash of cayenne (be careful), for adults

Combine all ingredients, except cayenne, in a large pot and simmer, covered, for about 30 minutes or more, to cook vegetables and blend flavors. (This cooking should reduce hotness of hot pepper and make this okay for kids.) Purée in blender or food processor. Reheat. Season to taste. Serve hot, with a tiny pinch of cayenne in cups for adults or pass cayenne separately.

Makes about 5 or 6 cups.

Basics

A s a helping hand, the following tidbits and odds and ends — soupçons, if you will — are simply a quick reference guide and some handy tips for success.

If you have time, make basic soup stock (the liquid base) from bones and vegetables and freeze it in 2-cup amounts to have on hand. But in case this can't be done, for lack of time or lack of space, try to keep canned chicken broth and canned beef broth or canned consomme on hand. They are excellent substitutes. As a real back-up, keep packaged instant dried chicken and beef broths in the cupboard. Remember that the quality of your soup will depend on the quality of your stock. To make a good soup with a thin watery stock is like trying to make a silk purse out of a sow's ear — it can't be done. And never forget that children can have just as discriminating palates as grown-ups. Maybe more so — adults might be polite and eat it anyway; kids won't, usually inheriting innate honesty at birth along with the afore-mentioned suspicious nature..

"Stock," "broth," and "bouillon" are fairly synonymous terms. Cook meat, bones, vegetables, and herbs with water for a time long enough to extract the good qualities from the ingredients. The cooking pot should be covered to prevent evaporation. And simmer — don't cook at a rolling boil and end up with an empty pot. A fair rule of thumb is a pound of meat, or meat and bones, and a quarter pound of vegetables to a quart of water.

Basic Beef Stock:

    3 to 4 pounds raw beef bones, with some meat on them
    water to cover them in a large pot
    ¼ teaspoon peppercorns
    4 cloves
    1 bay leaf
    1 carrot, sliced
    1 stalk celery, with leaves, cut up
    1 tablespoon salt
    ¼ teaspoon thyme
    ¼ teaspoon marjoram
    1 teaspoon parsley

Cover; heat slowly to boiling; reduce heat and simmer for about 3 hours. Strain; skim off fat; cool.

Basic Chicken Stock:

In a large kettle, in 4 tablespoons of vegetable oil or shortening, brown a 3- or 4-pound chicken, cut in pieces. (This browning is not obligatory, but it does produce a tastier stock.)
Add:

    3 quarts water
    1 carrot, cut up
    2 stalks celery, with leaves, cut up
    1 onion, sliced
    ¼ teaspoon peppercorns
    1 bay leaf
    1 tablespoon salt

Heat slowly to boiling; reduce heat and simmer until meat is very tender, at least an hour — better if longer. Strain; remove fat; cool.

Basic Vegetable Stock:

If you are a vegetarian, substitute vegetable stock for chicken or beef stock in the recipes. A pure vegetable stock can be made by simmering together, in a covered pot:

    2 carrots

    2 potatoes

    1 onion

    1 turnip

    2 tablespoons of dried peas or dried beans

    water to cover.

Any vegetable water (the liquid left when cooking vegetables) may be saved and used for a soup base.

Basic Consommé:

In a large kettle, brown 1 pound cubed beef in about a tablespoon of oil or butter, margarine, bacon fat, or some other shortening.
Add:

    2 more pounds beef, cubed

    a beef bone, such as a veal knuckle

    neck and giblets of 2 or 3 chickens

    4 quarts water

    1 tablespoon salt

    1 carrot, cut up

    1 onion, sliced

    1 stalk celery, with leaves, cut up

    1 turnip, cut up (optional)

    1 teaspoon peppercorns

    2 cloves

    bouquet garni (thyme, marjoram, parsley, and bay leaf)

Heat slowly to boiling; cover; reduce heat and simmer 3 hours or more. Strain; remove fat; cool.

Simple Garnishes

Garnishes are trimmings added to the soup as the final touch, for looks and a complementary taste. Use your imagination in selecting them.

- Almonds, blanched, shredded, and lightly toasted (for cream soups and chicken-based soups.)
- Avocado cubes or strips (for adults only; good with purées.)
- Chives, fresh or dried, (I chop and then freeze the ones from my garden) finely chopped. (Adults only; for creamy soups, especially ones with potatoes.)
- Grated fresh Parmesan or Romano or use dried cheese. Grated fresh cheeses will melt and get sticky on hot soups — stringy to eat, but good. (Use an extra dollop for kids: good with onion soup.)
- Croutons — store-bought or: remove crusts from bread slices and cut them into small cubes; toast in 350-degree oven for about 15 minutes to dry out, then toss in a little salted vegetable oil or melted butter and lightly brown in a frying pan. (Good with vegetable soups.)
- Hard-cooked Eggs, grated or sliced thin (for clear soups and purées.)
- Lemon or Orange, thinly sliced (for grown-ups and only for little ones with sophisticated tastes; great with clear soups.)
- Parsley, (or Basil, Mint, Watercress, etc.) — use the leaves and finely chop. (Adults only; good on anything.)
- Sour Cream — commercial brands, NOT soured cream. (Especially good with the dried bean and pea family and with tomato soups.)
- Sausage or Pepperoni — use cooked sausages cut into little bits or quartered pepperoni slices. (Good frankfurters, cooked and cut into bits, can also be tasty. Kids love them; excellent with vegetable soups.)
- Raw Vegetables — grated or minced carrots, celery, mushrooms, onion, etc. (Adults only; too alien on soup for kids; good with purées.)
- There was a time when people used a lightly salted spoon of whipped cream as a garnish, but this has become a no-no.

Odds and Ends of Terms

- Roux: A consistency made of vegetable oil or melted butter and flour in equal parts, then hot liquid added to form a thick creamy substance. This is the base for cream soups.
- Purée: In olden days, this was done by rubbing the ingredients through a sieve. I remember that in our kitchen in Georgia a perforated funnel-shaped colander with a pointed wooden pestle was used. Today, the food processor and the blender are invaluable. Puréed vegetables add thickening to coups without the calories of a roux.
- Cream Soups: These are bound together with a roux and milk or cream (namely a velouté sauce); or with a roux and stock; or with egg yolks and milk, cream, or stock.
- Bisque: This commonly means a thick soup with a purée base. It originally called for meat, especially fowl, as the main ingredient; then came shellfish as a substitute for the meat. Now vegetable bisques are standard.
- Potage: Another term for thick soup.

Helpful Hints

- If you have a microwave, it is very useful in heating stock or milk when soups call for adding heated liquids.
- Also, a microwave is useful if you are using frozen vegetables and want to use less than the package amount. Defrost package just enough that it can be broken up; take out desired amount. Refreeze rest.
- If a recipe calls for a certain herb and you don't have it, substitute, don't panic. One of the green leafy herbs can take the place of the missing one. Another example: If you need curry powder and are out, mix a little chili powder, ginger, and turmeric to use as a substitute. Mace can take the place of nutmeg. And so on. If in doubt, use only a very small amount and taste it to make a final decision.
- Above all, be brave. Cooking should be creative and fun. And the satisfaction of pleasing all ages is definitely rewarding.

Index

About the Author

Liza Fosburgh, a Southerner by birth, lives in the wooded Taconic Hills of New York. She has published numerous books of fiction, including award-winning novels for young adults, as well as nonfiction articles for magazines and newspapers. Her interests include cooking, gardening, and caring for several dogs and cats.